STERLING BIOGRAPHIES

AMELIA EARHART

A Life in Flight

Victoria Garrett Jones

STERLING

New York / London
www.sterlingpublishing.com/kids

In addition to my family, who endured seemingly endless Amelia stories with good humor, I would also like to thank my dear friend Missy Hollis, for her unfailing enthusiasm during this project. At Sterling, I am grateful to Kelly Smith, for her patience and encouragement, and to Susan Schader, for the many talents she brings to the photo selection process.

Finally, I would like to dedicate this volume to the memory of my mother, Lauretta Torrance Garrett, for whom no words can truly convey what is written on my heart.

STERLING and the distinctive Sterling logo are registered trademarks of Sterling Publishing Co., Inc.

Library of Congress Cataloging-in-Publication Data

Jones, Victoria Garrett.
   Amelia Earhart : a life in flight / by Victoria Garrett Jones.
      p. cm. — (Sterling biographies)
   Includes bibliographical references and index.
   ISBN 978-1-4027-5157-8 (pbk. : alk. paper) — ISBN 978-1-4027-6538-4 (hardcover : alk. paper)
   1. Earhart, Amelia, 1897-1937—Juvenile literature. 2. Women air pilots—United States—Biography—Juvenile literature. 3. Air pilots—United States—Biography—Juvenile literature. I. Title.
   TL540.E3J66 2009
   629.13092—dc22
   [B]
                                              2008029248

10 9 8 7 6 5 4 3 2 1

Published by Sterling Publishing Co., Inc.
387 Park Avenue South, New York, NY 10016
© 2009 by Victoria Garrett Jones
Distributed in Canada by Sterling Publishing
c/o Canadian Manda Group, 165 Dufferin Street
Toronto, Ontario, Canada M6K 3H6
Distributed in the United Kingdom by GMC Distribution Services
Castle Place, 166 High Street, Lewes, East Sussex, England BN7 1XU
Distributed in Australia by Capricorn Link (Australia) Pty. Ltd.
P.O. Box 704, Windsor, NSW 2756, Australia

Printed in China

Sterling ISBN 978-1-4027-5157-8 (paperback)
              978-1-4027-6538-4 (hardcover)

Image research by Larry Schwartz

For information about custom editions, special sales, premium and corporate purchases, please contact Sterling Special Sales Department at 800-805-5489 or specialsales@sterlingpublishing.com.

Contents

Events in the Life of Amelia Earhart

1897

July 24, 1897
Amelia Mary Earhart is born at her grandparents' home in Atchison, Kansas.

1908
At the Iowa State Fair, Amelia is unimpressed when she first sees an airplane.

February 1918
Shortly after leaving Philadelphia's Ogontz School, Amelia signs on as a nurse's aide at Toronto's Spadina Military Convalescent Hospital.

December 1920
Amelia has her first ride in an airplane, and she loves it.

January 3, 1921
With Neta Snook as her instructor, Amelia begins flying lessons. She buys her first airplane later that year.

October 1922
Amelia sets an unofficial women's altitude record of 14,000 feet.

June 1928
As a passenger aboard the *Friendship*, Amelia becomes the first woman to fly across the Atlantic Ocean.

August 1929
Even after stopping to assist a fellow pilot, Amelia takes third place in the first Women's Transcontinental Air Derby.

1930
Amelia is elected the first president of the Ninety-Nines, a newly-formed women's pilot organization.

February 7, 1931
Amelia marries publisher and promoter George Palmer Putnam.

April 8, 1931
The first woman to fly an autogiro, Amelia sets a long-standing altitude record of 18,415 feet in the new experimental aircraft.

May 21, 1932
Amelia becomes the first woman to fly solo across the Atlantic Ocean, and the first person to cross it twice by air.

August 1932
Flying from Los Angeles, California, to Newark, New Jersey, in just over nineteen hours, Amelia becomes the first woman pilot to fly nonstop from coast to coast.

January 1935
Amelia becomes the first person to make a solo flight from Honolulu, Hawaii, to Oakland, California.

April 1935
Amelia is the first person to fly solo from Los Angeles, California, to Mexico City, Mexico.

September 1, 1935
Amelia joins the faculty of Indiana's Purdue University as a career counselor for female students.

March 1937
Taking off from Oakland, California, Amelia begins her highly publicized, around-the-world flight. In Honolulu, Hawaii, an accident during takeoff temporarily halts her plans.

June 1, 1937
After her airplane is repaired, Amelia departs from Miami, Florida, for her second around-the-world attempt.

July 2, 1937
Amelia, along with navigator Fred Noonan, disappears in the Pacific somewhere near Howland Island.

January 5, 1939
Amelia Earhart is declared legally dead.

1939

A Woman of Courage

Courage is the price that Life exacts for granting peace.

Many hours of flying in darkness, fog, thunder, and ice had gone by when Amelia Earhart first noticed the steady drip . . . drip . . . drip of gasoline falling onto her left shoulder and running down her neck. Perhaps even more perilous was the blue flame flickering from her aircraft's engine, which she could see just outside her cockpit window. In her quest to become the first woman to fly alone across the Atlantic Ocean, Amelia knew she faced grave danger. Many others—both men and women— had died trying to do what she was attempting. Amelia wondered whether her small plane would be able to endure several more hours of brutal battering by the wind and bad weather before she might glimpse land. Would she successfully accomplish her goal or perish in the dark Atlantic waters below?

Knowing the risks but taking the chance was the internal compass that guided the direction of Amelia Earhart's life and accomplishments. "Women must try to do things as men have tried," she once wrote. "When they fail, their failure must be but a challenge to others." Although her own story ended much too quickly, the course that Amelia set in her life forged a path that gave women everywhere the chance to reach previously undreamed of goals.

CHAPTER 1

Kansas Roots

I am sure I was a horrid little girl . . . perhaps the fact that I was exceedingly fond of reading made me endurable.

In 1897, as America stood poised on the brink of a new century, Atchison, Kansas, was ranked as an important midwestern center of commerce and trade. It was here on July 24 that Amelia Mary Earhart was born in the home of her maternal grandparents, Alfred and Amelia Otis. Named for both her grandmothers—Amelia Otis and Mary

Amelia Mary Earhart, dressed in christening finery, poses for her first photograph in 1897.

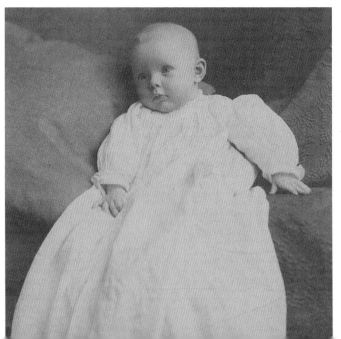

Earhart—Amelia made her appearance not long before midnight, and weighed a healthy nine pounds. She was the first of two daughters born to Edwin and Amy Earhart. The second, Grace Muriel, was born in 1899 in Kansas City.

Courtship and Marriage

Amy's family was wealthy and socially prominent. Her father, a judge, was highly respected in the community. Amy, the eldest daughter, was popular and pretty. It was at her well-attended **coming-out ball** that she met Edwin Stanton Earhart, a young lawyer.

Edwin's background was quite different from Amy's. His father was a Lutheran minister, and his family lived in a near-constant state of poverty. Edwin, the youngest child, grew up facing hardship and sacrifice. After attending college on a Lutheran scholarship, Edwin taught school for a few years before studying law at Kansas State University, where he earned money for his tuition by tutoring other students and assisting various professors.

Amy and Edwin began seeing each other frequently after the coming-out ball and soon fell in love. But Judge Otis was not sure about Edwin's prospects for the future. After waiting five years for Edwin to achieve a salary level required by Amy's father, the couple was married in Atchison on October 16, 1895. As a wedding gift, Amy's parents gave the newlyweds a fully furnished house in Kansas City, where Edwin practiced law with a partner, J. E. Barker.

Married life was something of a shock for Amy—particularly the change in her income level and social status—but she was determined to make the best of things and soon settled into her new life. Unfortunately, Edwin was not responsible with money.

Financial difficulties shadowed the young couple almost from the beginning of their marriage, which seemed to confirm Judge Otis's feelings about his son-in-law's worthlessness. Despite the couple's ongoing financial problems and the ever-deepening rift between her husband and her father, Amy sent three-year-old Amelia to visit her parents in Atchison shortly after Muriel's birth. Amy's mother had recently lost several family members and took comfort from being with her granddaughter and namesake. Eventually it was decided that Amelia would live in Atchison with her grandparents during the school year and return to her parents' home in Kansas City during the summers. Amy and Muriel visited often, and Amelia thrived at her grandparents' home where she was surrounded by family and friends.

A Young and Daring Spirit

As Amelia grew up, she became known for her cleverness and daring. Quick to organize others for games and adventures, Amelia was very popular. The friends she made during these years in Atchison remained close to her throughout her entire life. Recognizing her daughters' tomboy spirit, Amy Earhart had

bloomer-style play clothes made for both Amelia and Muriel. These came in handy during some of their childhood exploits. Both "Meelie" and "Pidge" (as Amelia and Muriel affectionately called each other) were encouraged in their athletic pursuits. In a childhood Christmas letter, Amelia wrote, "Dear Dad: Muriel and I would like footballs this year, please. We need them specially, as we have plenty of baseballs, bats, etc."

Following a 1904 visit to the **World's Fair** in St. Louis, Amelia decided to build a roller coaster in her grandparents' backyard. After selecting the eight-foot-high roof of a toolshed as a good starting point, she organized neighborhood children and her cousins into a construction team. Using two-by-fours, a kitchen stepladder, packing boxes, tools, and nails, the elevated track took shape.

Amelia greased the wood boards with lard, climbed onto the roof, squeezed herself into an open packing crate, and took off. Traveling much faster than anticipated, she raced past the other children in a blur. The ride ended abruptly with the sound of splintering wood. Sporting a torn dress and bruised lip, Amelia immediately made plans for repairs and redesign. Her mother's prompt appearance, however, put a stop to the plans, and the roller coaster was dismantled amid protests from all.

In this c. 1904 photograph, Amelia clutches a toy lamb as she and her younger sister Muriel sit on the steps of their Kansas City home.

Amelia's birthplace in Atchison, Kansas, boasts a model of the homemade roller coaster she constructed following a visit to the 1904 World's Fair.

While living in Atchison, Amelia became the proud owner of a boy's sled—a gift from her father. In winter, while the other girls sat upright on their sleds, Amelia would lie flat as she coasted down hills. During one sledding expedition, she found herself sailing down a particularly icy slope and directly into the path of a junk man's horse-drawn cart. Unable to stop and her yells unheard by the driver, Amelia—head down—was miraculously able to slip directly between the front and rear legs of the surprised horse.

A First Glimpse of Flying

In 1908, Edwin, unsuccessful in his law practice, accepted a position with the Rock Island Railroad line as a **claims agent**. Although the job promised a potential improvement in the Earharts' finances, it also meant moving the family to Des Moines, Iowa, thereby ending Amelia's school-year residency with her grandparents.

It was in Iowa at the 1908 State Fair where Amelia saw an airplane for the first time. She was completely unimpressed. Later she would write that it was "a thing of rusty wire and wood and looked not at all interesting." Fewer than five years had

Flight at Kitty Hawk

Wilbur and Orville Wright later credited their early interest in aviation to a childhood helicopter toy that was brought home by their father, a minister, who encouraged the boys' curiosity about mechanical things. By 1899, the brothers had begun experiments in aircraft research—initially involving kites, then man-sized gliders, and eventually engine-powered aircraft. In order to conduct extensive trials and flight testing, they needed just the right location. Searching for a site that would offer strong, steady winds and plenty of space for maneuverability, they settled on the small Atlantic coast fishing village of Kitty Hawk, North Carolina. The area's large sand dunes also provided the cushion needed to make relatively low-impact landings.

On December 17, 1903, after four years of experimentation, the Wright brothers made history on the dunes of Kitty Hawk. They had designed—and successfully flown—the world's first heavier-than-air, powered aircraft able to make a controlled and sustained flight with a pilot on board. Although the maximum distance flown was only 852 feet and the greatest time aloft less than a minute (59 seconds), the feat's impact on mankind was incredible.

In 1903, Wilbur and Orville Wright made aviation history on the dunes of Kitty Hawk, North Carolina.

passed since the Wright brothers made history on the dunes of Kitty Hawk, and aviation as we know it today was still in its infancy. The "aeroplane" Amelia saw on that bright summer day was probably a biplane (having two sets of wings). Its somewhat unusual structure required that the engine and wooden propeller be mounted in the rear, while the pilot sat up front in a birdcage-like seat. Little did eleven-year-old Amelia know that she was glimpsing her destiny.

Happy Times for the Earharts

At first the move to Des Moines seemed a blessing for the Earharts. In addition to nearly doubling Edwin's salary, the position also brought other benefits, including a cook and a maid. A private railroad car meant the Earharts were now able to travel in style on their return trips to visit the Otis family in Atchison.

Writing later in life, Amelia recalled happy evenings when her father would read aloud or tell fascinating stories he made up on the spot. Both shared a love of music—especially the piano. As a family, the Earharts attended formal concerts at the Drake Conservatory of Music. Afterward, Edwin and Amelia would attempt to play the music they'd heard performed on stage earlier in the evening. On weekends, Edwin was always available as the "Big Chief" for games of cowboys and Indians with his daughters and their friends. He took the girls fishing on the Des Moines River, and the family enjoyed lakeside holidays in Minnesota.

Edwin's "Sickness"

It was around this time, when things seemed the best and the brightest for the Earhart family, that Edwin began a downward slide into alcoholism, and his behavior became more and more erratic. Although Amelia would never publicly refer to her father's drinking problem, her sister Muriel later wrote about the impact their father's "sickness" had on the family.

Muriel recalled one particular Saturday afternoon when she and a large group of neighborhood children eagerly awaited Edwin's arrival home. As he got off the streetcar, Muriel and Amelia immediately sensed something was wrong. "He walked slowly, putting each foot down carefully as if to keep from stumbling. . . . We escorted him home in a curious silence, and he lurched up the steps." Edwin Earhart was drunk.

Writing later in life, Amelia recalled happy evenings when her father would read aloud or tell fascinating stories he made up on the spot.

The situation only worsened. Soon it was apparent to Edwin's coworkers that his problem was quite serious. Eventually he was told to seek help or he would lose his job. A month's hospitalization brought some hope to Amy and her daughters, but the respite was brief.

The death of Amy's parents brought further hardship to the Earhart family. Alfred and Amelia Otis had left Amy's share of their considerable fortune locked in a trust that was largely untouchable for twenty years or until Edwin's death, whichever came first. At this final insult from his in-laws, Edwin began drinking heavily again, which led to his release from the Rock Island Railroad line.

As Amelia entered her teens, it became more and more apparent that her parents' marriage was no longer a happy one. Sadly, Edwin's constant financial troubles and battle with alcoholism would soon split the family apart.

CHAPTER 2

Walking Alone

A single act of kindness throws out roots in all directions, and the roots spring up and make new trees.

After months of searching, Edwin finally found a job as a low-ranking freight clerk with the Great Northern Railroad in St. Paul, Minnesota. Amelia and Muriel, though sorry to leave their friends and schoolmates behind, saw the move as an adventure and wondered what might lie ahead. Reflecting back on her family's many moves some years later, Amelia wrote, "I have never lived more than four years in any one place and always have to ask 'Which one?' when a stranger greets me by saying, 'I'm from your home town.'"

Living in St. Paul

In St. Paul the Earharts rented a large, drafty house that proved nearly impossible to heat. Coal was expensive and money was scarce, so the family lived in only two rooms during the winter months. To save money, Amy and her daughters would walk three miles to the market instead of spending money on the fare for a streetcar. Yet Edwin continued to drink. Once, Edwin caught Amelia pouring a bottle of whiskey down the sink, and he yelled at his daughter to stop. It was likely that only Amy's sudden appearance kept him from hitting Amelia. Increasingly he disappointed or embarrassed his oldest child. Amelia

Amelia, shown here at age ten, moved frequently during the later years of her childhood as financial worries and her father's instability shadowed the Earhart family.

became very protective of her mother and sister—a habit that would strengthen as she grew older.

While in St. Paul, Amelia—a junior—attended Central High School, where she made good grades and played on the girls' basketball team. Her favorite subjects included mathematics and Latin. Due to their financial circumstances, the Earhart family's social life was nearly nonexistent. St. Clement's Episcopal Church became a focal point for Amy and her daughters. Muriel sang in the choir, and Amelia joined the Altar Guild.

On the Move Again

After only a year in St. Paul, Edwin announced he had found yet another job—this time in Springfield, Missouri. The position supposedly included some legal work and the possibility of advancement. With no choice but to accompany him, Amy and her daughters packed their belongings once more. "Moving hurts more in the heart of a teenager than it does at any other age," wrote Muriel years later. "The telephone, which had been silent for months, was just beginning to ring for us. We would not be there to answer."

Once in Springfield, the Earharts again faced disappointment. There was no job for Edwin. The man he was supposed to replace had decided not to retire. This was the final straw for Amy.

Accompanied by her daughters, Amy moved to Chicago to live with friends of the family until she could find an apartment. Edwin traveled alone to stay with his elderly sister in Kansas City. Little indication was given of when—or if—the family would be reunited. Once in Chicago, Amelia steered her mother toward the district with the best public high school—Hyde Park.

At seventeen, Amelia was tall and very thin, with wide-set bluish-gray eyes and high cheekbones. With quiet determination, she set about obtaining the best scientific education possible within her family's financial limitations. Unlike her junior year in St. Paul when she had participated in various activities, Amelia made no attempt to fit in. She entered Hyde Park High School as an outsider and remained so throughout her entire senior year. The space next to her yearbook photo, where student activities were normally listed, was left blank. Her photo was captioned "the girl in brown who walks alone." Although she completed her senior year satisfactorily, she did not attend her graduation, pick up her diploma, or go to the senior banquet. She had been enrolled in six high schools in four years; rather than living in the present, she was looking to the future.

Little indication was given of when—or if—the family would be reunited.

After ten months in Chicago, Amy made the decision to move to Kansas City and try to reunite the family. Edwin Earhart, practicing law once more, seemed to have stopped drinking. Edwin persuaded Amy to challenge her parents' wills. She was successful and decided to put part of the sizable sum she received toward her daughters' education. Muriel would go to St. Margaret's College in Toronto, while Amelia would head east to attend the Ogontz School outside Philadelphia.

Attending Ogontz School

While providing a decent enough education for its students, Ogontz had more of a **finishing school** reputation than that of a serious academic institution. Amy may have looked at Ogontz as a way to reestablish Amelia's social standing. Whatever the reasons, Muriel headed to Toronto and nineteen-year-old Amelia went to Philadelphia.

Little has been published about the time Amelia spent at Ogontz. Years later, she gave the school only a brief mention in her autobiography, *The Fun of It*. Still, school records and family letters indicate that Amelia arrived in October of 1916, and that her studies included French, German, composition, economics, and geometry. Overall, her grades were quite good, and she excelled in field hockey and basketball.

Unlike her self-imposed isolation at Hyde Park High School, Amelia quickly became very popular at Ogontz. She served on the student honor board, was voted class vice president, and was selected to write the senior song. She also appeared to enjoy herself more, and a sense of fun, which had been missing for some time, returned to her life. In one letter to her mother she wrote about playing ukuleles with friends until midnight. The girls made hot chocolate with marshmallows and "drank it out of trophy cups." Distance from family sorrows and

Dressed in her cap and gown during the fall of her senior year at Ogontz, Amelia left the Philadelphia area school before graduating.

disappointments no doubt helped lighten Amelia's spirits, and she seemed to thrive.

While Amelia was at Ogontz, Amy Earhart's sister and brother-in-law, Margaret and Clarence Balis, stepped in to watch over their niece. They lived with their five children just a few miles from the school's campus. Amelia was very fond of her relatives and spent semester breaks at the Balis family home. Occasionally Margaret was summoned to Ogontz when her niece had gotten into a jam. For example, Amelia had always been very fond of climbing. Having lost none of her childhood sense of daring and adventure, she continued this practice while at Ogontz—often on the roofs of school buildings. Unfortunately, the headmistress did not share her enthusiasm.

Becoming a Young Woman

It was around this time that Amelia began to gather newspaper clippings and various magazine articles into a scrapbook that she entitled "Activities of Women." Enclosed were stories of those with interesting and varied careers—a police commissioner, a city manager, a forestry service fire lookout, a bank president, an engineer, a film producer, an attorney—all were women, all were achievers.

During the summer following her first year at Ogontz, Amelia vacationed with school friends, and she spent little time at home. Boys were beginning to notice the tall and willowy beauty. Returning to Ogontz that fall, Amelia seemed uncertain about a future there despite her popularity with fellow students.

Boys were beginning to notice the tall and willowy beauty.

Letters home indicate that she was maturing, and the tone of her writing was more thoughtful and serious. "What do you think of the railroad strike and the abdication of the Tzar?" she wrote to her mother after Nicholas II left the Russian throne. World events were filtering through to her relatively sheltered world. Immersed in academic studies and school social activities, Amelia and her fellow students had little grasp of the enormous changes taking place in the world around them. World War I—the Great War— had been raging in Europe since 1914, and in April of 1917, the United States had entered the conflict.

Working for the Cause in Toronto

Although Amelia had helped to knit sweaters for soldiers and raise money for the Red Cross while in school, visiting her mother and Muriel in Toronto for Christmas in 1917 was an eye-opener. Unlike the United States, Canada had been involved in the war since its beginning, and the conflict's harsh realities were obvious everywhere. "There for the first time I realized what the World War meant," Amelia wrote in her autobiography. "Instead of new uniforms and brass bands, I saw only the results of four years' desperate struggle; men without arms and legs, men who were paralyzed, and men who were blind."

Amelia came away from the experience overwhelmed by what she had seen and returned to

WHAT are YOU doing to HELP?

Gordon Grant — JOIN YOUR
AMERICAN RED CROSS
Subscribing Memberships $2.00 up

Still in its infancy when World War I began, the Red Cross experienced tremendous growth during the terrible conflict. Amelia was among the millions who served during wartime.

World War I (1914–1918)

Referred to by many historians as "the war to end all wars," this monumental conflict claimed the lives of some ten million men. Beginning with the assassination of Austria's Archduke Franz Ferdinand in the Bosnian capital of Sarajevo, the nations of the world entered into a bitter struggle that pitted the Allied Powers (primarily Great Britain, France, Italy, Belgium, Russia, and eventually the United States) against the Central Powers (mainly Bulgaria, Austria-Hungary, the Ottoman Empire [modern-day Turkey], and Germany).

Unprecedented in terms of death, destruction, and overall scale, the war also brought recent technological advances into military use, such as the tank, submarine, and airplane. The defeat of the Central Powers and the signing of the Treaty of Versailles on June 28, 1919, marked the end of four huge empires—the Russian, German, Ottoman, and Austro-Hungarian—and left postwar Europe facing widespread economic hardship.

French soldiers stage an assault on German positions in Champagne, France, in 1917.

Ogontz a changed person. She found that she could not wipe these sights from her mind and continue her studies. She had to do something constructive. She had to *act*. By February, Amelia returned to Toronto and joined the **Volunteer Aid Detachment**. After completing a Red Cross first aid course, Amelia began working as a nurse's aide and was eventually assigned to Spadina Military Convalescent Hospital. The shifts were long and grueling—twelve hours with a two-hour break in the afternoon.

Despite the rigors of her schedule, Amelia found the work rewarding and her new sense of personal freedom exhilarating. When she was not at the hospital, her social life was busy with concerts, sporting events, dinners out, and plenty of admirers. When Muriel could join Amelia, the two sisters often rented horses from a local stable and went riding together. One mount named Dynamite was a favorite of Amelia's. Treated poorly by a previous owner, Dynamite had been extremely mistrustful of humans. But with calming

Amelia's love of riding continued throughout her life, which is evident in this photo from the 1930s.

words, gentle pats, and juicy apples, Amelia was able to win him over. The stable owner was so appreciative of Amelia's efforts that Dynamite was hers to ride whenever she wished, at no charge. As luck would have it, this horse would—indirectly—reintroduce Amelia to airplanes and the wonder of flight, forever changing the course of her life.

CHAPTER 3

Finding Her Wings

Experiment! Meet new people! . . . That's better than any college education.

A number of the wounded soldiers whom Amelia cared for at Spadina Hospital were pilots—mostly British and French. No doubt Amelia heard about their adventures in the air while she was tending to their injuries. In addition, a group of officers from the Royal Flying Corps often rode horses at the same rental stables as Amelia.

Impressed with the patience and courage she had displayed in gentling the nervous horse Dynamite, one officer—Captain Spaulding—asked if Amelia and Muriel would like to come out to the airfield to watch him fly. They eagerly accepted, but were disappointed to learn that they were forbidden by military regulations from going for a ride. Still, Amelia was impressed with the display of flying skills she saw that day.

A Fascination with Flying

In fact, Amelia was so impressed that she began visiting the airfield whenever she could to watch the pilots' training maneuvers. Most of the military pilots trained in an aircraft called the Curtiss Jenny, and Amelia was eager to learn about it and aviation in general. "I hung around in [my] spare time and absorbed all I could," she later recalled.

The Curtiss Jenny

One of the most popular planes in the early days of aviation, the Curtiss JN-4, or "Jenny," served as a training aircraft for nearly ninety-five percent of all American and Canadian pilots during World War I. Although these two-seater biplanes never saw military action, British and French air schools also used them for some of their pilots' training.

After the war, the well-known Jenny was a favorite of civilians learning to fly and a featured sight at air shows where stunt flyers called "barnstormers" dazzled crowds with daring feats like wing-walking, dangerous spins, and midair acrobatics. The first plane of Charles Lindbergh, who later gained fame with his transatlantic flight in the *Spirit of St. Louis*, was a Curtiss Jenny, which he purchased for $500 in 1923. And it was in a Canadian version of the Jenny, the Curtiss "Canuck," that Amelia Earhart first took flying lessons. Unable to keep up with rapidly advancing aviation technology, the Curtiss Jenny's fate was sealed when it failed to meet new U.S. government safety regulations in the late 1920s.

Although never flown in battle, the Curtiss Jenny saw plenty of stateside service. In 1923, Charles Lindbergh made his first solo flight in a JN-4.

Dressed in riding garb with her long hair pinned up out of the way, Amelia strikes a casual pose for this photo taken in Canada around 1918.

While in Toronto, Amelia and a friend had the opportunity to attend an exhibition of stunt flying at the local fairgrounds. Standing in the middle of a field, they had a great view of the action above. As Amelia relayed the story later, one pilot—probably bored with performing the rolls, spins, and loops that were the standard fare of the stunt flyer—spotted the two young women and decided to have some fun. Speeding steadily downward, the plane began to head straight for the two spectators. Amelia held her ground while her friend ran to safety. "Common sense told me if something went wrong . . . the airplane and I would be rolled up in a ball together," she reflected. However, she continued to watch, fascinated, as the pilot pulled the plane up and away without a moment to spare. Amelia was hooked. "I believe that little red airplane said something to me as it swished by," she later recalled. Although Amelia continued her work at the hospital, she could not put her fascination with airplanes aside.

A Long and Painful Illness

As the war came to a close, Amelia was still in Toronto. But by the time **Armistice Day** arrived on November 11, 1918, she was seriously ill. The long hours of work with little sleep and the stress of caring for so many critically ill patients had taken its toll. She developed a severe sinus infection—some thought she had pneumonia as well—and was hospitalized. Amelia was subjected to a series of painful treatments that required a lengthy recovery period.

As a result of her illness, sinus problems would continue to plague her throughout the rest of her life. The extreme discomfort and near-constant pain, especially after some of her longer flights, required several surgeries, but Amelia did not complain. Little mention is made of her condition in her letters and other writings.

When she was well enough to travel, Amelia joined Muriel, who had transferred from St. Margaret's and was now a student at Smith College in Northampton, Massachusetts. Quickly bored by the lack of activity, Amelia taught herself how to play the banjo and enrolled in an automobile engine repair class. After spending the next summer vacationing at New York's Lake George with her mother and sister, Amelia began to think

Although Amelia continued her work at the hospital, she could not put her fascination with airplanes aside.

about medicine as a possible career. She had found nursing rewarding and wanted to do something that would make a difference. Not wanting to waste any time, Amelia—now age twenty-two—moved to New York that fall and began taking premed classes at Columbia University. "It took me only a few months," she later wrote, "to discover that I probably should not make the ideal physician."

Rejoining the Family

By this time, Edwin and Amy were living in California. Edwin had stopped drinking and was clearly trying to make an attempt to reunite the family, but the Earhart marriage was in trouble. Although reluctant, Amelia headed west to be with her parents, arriving in Los Angeles, California, in the summer of 1920. In order to help pay the rent on their modest home, Amy and Edwin had taken in three young men as boarders. One of them, Sam Chapman, was an attractive young chemical engineer. Finding they shared many similar interests, such as swimming, tennis, and reading, he and Amelia became good friends and began to spend a great deal of time together.

As was her habit while in Toronto, Amelia began to visit local airfields and air shows to watch and to learn. That December, Edwin made arrangements for Amelia to ride in a plane for the first time. The ten-minute flight cost ten dollars (which equals about one hundred dollars today). The pilot, Frank Hawks, was uncertain about having a woman passenger aboard. Fearing that Amelia might try to jump out or try some other ridiculous act while they were in the air, Hawks arranged to have a second pilot fly with them. Despite being put off by this **chauvinistic** attitude, Amelia was completely and utterly captivated. "As soon as we left the ground I knew I myself had to fly," she later wrote. When she told her parents about her decision, her father objected to the cost of lessons. Edwin thought that this would put an end to Amelia's interest, but he was dead wrong. She immediately went out and got a job with the telephone company in order to pay for flying lessons.

In this photo, taken more than a decade after their initial encounter, Amelia shares a laugh with pilot Frank Hawks, who took her for her first airplane ride in 1920.

Learning to Fly

Not wanting to take lessons with Frank Hawks, who was less than enthusiastic about women flying, Amelia set out to find a female instructor. Despite Edwin's initial reluctance to the whole idea, he accompanied his daughter. Although the number of women pilots was small, the names of flyers such as Baroness de la Roche and Harriet Quimby had already appeared in the news. At Kinner Field, Amelia met Anita "Neta" Snook, a woman pilot just a year older than she was.

Neta had been the first woman to graduate from the Curtiss School of Aviation. In addition to giving lessons, she did **aerial advertising** and carried passengers throughout the Los Angeles area. Standing just a little over five feet in height, Neta had the

Shown here wearing the standard pilot's "uniform" of leather coat and high boots, Anita "Neta" Snook was Amelia's first flying instructor.

personality to match her bright red hair. Amelia would write to Muriel about Neta, "She dresses and talks like a man and can do everything around a plane that a man can do. I'm lucky that she'll teach me." The two young women agreed on a lesson price of a dollar a minute for Amelia's instruction time, which was to be paid at the end of each day's session.

On January 3, 1921, the future pilot arrived for her first day of lessons dressed in boots and well-worn, but still beautiful, tailored riding clothes, with a book on **aerodynamics** in her hand. In those early days of flying, pants were a necessity for women because planes did not have doors. A pilot had to climb up the side and swing a leg over into the open cockpit to get in.

Neta Snook's plane was a Canadian version of the Curtiss Jenny biplane known as a Canuck. The plane had two open cockpits—each identical to the other in terms of instruments and steering. Once the plane was in the air, a hand-controlled stick made the plane go up or down—pushing forward on the stick made the plane's nose go down, while pulling back on it sent the nose upward. Steering was accomplished by the use of a foot-controlled rudder bar, which turned the plane like a steering wheel turns a car.

As the instructor operated the controls in the rear cockpit, the controls in the student's front cockpit moved the same way. Everything else was quite basic—there was no rear wheel, no brakes, and no gas gauge. The body or "skin" of the Canuck was made from linen panels that had been sewn, stretched, and then shrunk onto the frame. The Canuck was slow to climb, underpowered, and hard to keep level, making it difficult to fly. After just a few hours of flying lessons, Amelia knew enough to realize that she did not like Neta's plane.

Amelia's first flying lessons took place in a twin-seated Curtiss "Canuck," similar to the aircraft shown here. Dual controls with identical features were used for pilot instruction.

Prominent Women Aviators
of the Early Twentieth Century

During the early history of flight, there were a handful of successful women flyers. Baroness Raymonde de la Roche (1886–1919) was one of them. Taught to fly by the famous French aviator and plane designer Charles Voisin, la Roche qualified for an F.A.I. (Fédération Aéronautique Internationale—the world air sports organization) pilot's license—the first such license granted to a woman—in fewer than six months. In 1913, she went on to win the Aero Club of France's Femina Cup

Baroness Raymonde de la Roche sits in her Voisin biplane in 1909.

for a four-hour nonstop flight. Six years later, while a passenger on an aircraft's flight test, she was killed when the plane crashed on its landing approach. A statue at La Bourget Airport near Paris commemorates la Roche's career as an aviation pioneer.

Harriet Quimby (1875–1912) was a popular figure in early U.S. aviation history. She became fascinated with flying in 1910, and after just four months, she became the first American woman to obtain a pilot's license in August 1911. The following month, she became the first woman to make a nighttime flight, and in April 1912, Harriet became the first female pilot to cross the English Channel—from Dover, England, to Hardelot, France. Harriet's career was tragically cut short when she was thrown from her plane during an air meet near Boston, Massachusetts, on July 1, 1912.

In 1911, Harriet Quimby became the first American woman to obtain a pilot's license.

Amelia's First Airplane

By the time Amelia turned twenty-four in the summer of 1921, she had managed to buy her own aircraft. Although Amelia was still working as a clerk at the telephone company, her salary was not enough to cover her aviation expenses. Eventually she took a second job driving a gravel truck. Seeing Amelia's determination to pursue flying, her family also provided their support—financially as well as emotionally. Amelia's first plane was a Kinner Airster. Lighter, easier to maintain, and more responsive than the less graceful Canuck, the little plane was speedy and attractive. Its engine was air-cooled—a new invention—which made the plane lighter and easier to maneuver. She named her plane the *Canary* because of its bright yellow color. "It was like a favorite pony," Amelia's mother later recalled. "We said goodnight to it and patted its nose and almost fed it apples."

Amelia had begun to look the part of an aviator. In addition to a helmet and goggles, she had bought a long leather coat.

Standing in front of Amelia's Kinner Airster in 1921, Neta Snook (left) poses with her famous pupil. Amelia dubbed her plane the *Canary* because of its bright yellow color.

Thinking it looked too new, Amelia wore it everywhere for several days—even sleeping in it at night—to give the coat a more "aged" appearance. It was around this time that Amelia also made the decision to cut her waist-length hair.

Aware that women flyers were considered unusual or eccentric by much of the general public, Amelia had been reluctant to switch to an easy-to-care-for "bob" (short haircut). At that time, few women wore their hair short. But when a young girl had commented that Amelia didn't look like an aviator due to her long hair, Amelia took the plunge.

Although Amelia had had enough ground instruction and hours in the air to fly solo, she wanted to learn about stunt flying and began to take lessons from John "Monte" Montijo, an ex-Army pilot. This was not due to any desire to entertain at air shows, but because Amelia wanted to have confidence in her ability to handle her plane if something went wrong during a flight. "It seemed foolhardy to try to go up alone without the ability to recognize and recover quickly from any position the plane might assume," she later wrote. Over the next several months, Amelia learned loops and barrel rolls, tailspins and dives—all the tricks of the stunt flyer's trade—until they became second nature to her. Before the end of the year, she was ready to take the next big step—her first solo flight.

Wanting to be taken seriously as a pilot, Amelia decided to cut her waist-length hair. This photo of the youthful flyer appeared on an early pilot's license.

CHAPTER 4

A Solo Flyer

My first solo had come and gone without anything to mark it but an exceptionally poor landing.

Amelia's first solo flight ended almost before it began. A shock absorber broke off during takeoff, causing the plane's left wing to sag. Amelia quickly returned to the ground for repairs. Once the plane was fixed, she took off again. Soaring to five thousand feet, she flew for a bit and then returned to the ground.

On December 15, 1921, Amelia passed a two-part test that was a qualification needed for eventually obtaining an F.A.I. license (Fédération Aéronautique Internationale). For the first part of the test, Amelia had to demonstrate her ability to make a "dead-stick landing." Taking her plane up to nearly five thousand feet, Amelia had to turn off the engine and then glide downward to land within about five hundred feet of a marked location—all without restarting the engine.

For the second part of the test, Amelia had to fly five figure-eight courses around a series of posts set in the ground—all at less than seven hundred feet in the air. When she was finished, she had to land her plane within 164 feet of a given spot. Accomplishing all of this took skill and composure. When Amelia was granted a license from the National Aeronautic Association, she was only the sixteenth woman in the world to receive one.

Early Mishaps in the Sky

Amelia's early aviation experiences were not entirely without mishaps. Her first crash occurred when she was still Neta Snook's student. Heading down a runway for takeoff, Amelia realized that her plane wasn't gaining altitude fast enough to clear a grove of trees at the end. Rather than slam into the trees, Amelia chose to hit the softer ground and crashed directly into a cabbage patch. Fortunately, damaged landing gear and a broken propeller were the only casualties. Neta was impressed by Amelia's calm as her student quickly cut the engine's power switch to prevent fire and then began to powder her nose. "We have to look nice when the reporters come," was Amelia's only comment.

On another occasion, Amelia had become disoriented while flying in thick fog and sleet. Fearful that the plane's wings would begin to ice up and cause a crash, she knew she needed to get out of the situation as quickly as she could. She put the plane into a spin so she could rapidly descend into warmer air. Fortunately, Amelia was able to get out

Her first crash occurred when she was still Neta Snook's student.

of the poor weather and pull out of the dangerous spin while she was still several thousand feet up in the air. After she landed, male pilots on the ground criticized her decision to take such a chance. Had she not pulled out of the spin, they cautioned, they'd have been digging pieces of Amelia and her plane out of the ground. "Yes, I suppose you would," was her cool reply.

Beginning to Set Records

Amelia continued to fly solo whenever she had enough money to pay for fuel. In addition, she participated in a few "air rodeos" at Kinner and other area airfields. Though Amelia was not

Air shows were extremely popular with spectators, as indicated by the packed stands in this 1920s-era photo. Many pilots, including Amelia, performed in these shows to help pay for maintenance costs and fuel for their airplanes.

particularly interested in impressing air show crowds, the money she earned helped to pay for her aviation expenses and, as a female pilot, she was also aware of the publicity factor. In nearly all of her future endeavors, Amelia tried to promote the abilities of women.

For one particular show held at Los Angeles's Rogers Air Field in October of 1922, Amelia made certain there were tickets on hand for her father and sister. She was somewhat mysterious about her reasons for wanting her family members to attend. Edwin and Muriel soon found out why once they were seated in the spectator stands and spotted Amelia on the field.

As she climbed into her Kinner biplane, an announcement was made that Amelia was going to try to set a new altitude record. After a smooth takeoff, her plane disappeared in the clouds. For nearly an hour, while spectators were entertained by other exhibitions of flying skills held closer to the ground, Edwin and Muriel scanned the skies for a glimpse of the little yellow plane. Finally Amelia appeared, landed safely, and was soon surrounded by a group of officials. Shortly thereafter, a loudspeaker announced that Amelia had flown to an altitude of fourteen thousand feet—a new unofficial women's record. Although the record was broken just a few weeks later by Ruth Nichols—another talented female pilot—the experience still marked Amelia's *first* "first" in aviation record-setting.

Amelia's friend and competitor Ruth Nichols set numerous women's aviation records. Two years after this 1929 photo was taken, Ruth made her first of two unsuccessful attempts to cross the Atlantic alone.

More Family Problems

Although these years brought much satisfaction to Amelia in her efforts as an aviator, Amelia knew that her mother's inheritance had been rapidly dwindling and that her aviation expenses contributed to her parents' financial situation. She hoped to remedy things by encouraging Amy and Edwin to invest in a small Nevada gypsum (a mineral most commonly used in plaster of paris) mine owned by a friend. While the investment had seemed sound, a flash flood wiped out everything—and nearly all of the Earharts' remaining funds.

With no money to pay for her education, Muriel dropped out of Smith, returned to her parents' home, and began teaching English at a local school. Amelia, burdened by guilt over the entire episode, sold her plane and took on additional jobs—including work in a local photography studio—to help with family expenses. Sam Chapman, still a boarder at the Earhart

Sam Chapman, a boarder at the Earharts' Los Angeles home, sits to the right of Amelia in this undated photo. The attractive young engineer proposed marriage in 1924.

home, became even closer to Amelia at this time, and the young couple began to talk about marriage and a future together.

By January of 1924, it became apparent that Amy and Edwin Earhart's marriage was at an end. After nearly thirty years together, they made the decision to divorce. Rather than stay in California, Amy and her daughters decided to move east. Muriel enrolled in summer school at Harvard and left first by train. Amelia, suffering again from serious sinus problems, could not travel right away, and Amy stayed behind with her older daughter. Even though Amelia hoped to one day travel across the country by air, for now she purchased a bright yellow Kissell touring car—later nicknamed the "Yellow Peril"—and drove cross-country with her mother as her passenger.

Taking their time, they made many stops along the way, visiting Yosemite, Oregon's Crater Lake, Lake Louise and the town of Banff in Canada, Yellowstone National Park, and other scenic spots. During the last part of the trip, Amelia's sinus infection returned. Three days after arriving in Boston, she was back in the hospital for yet another procedure. This time a small piece of bone was removed to allow her sinuses to drain properly. Fortunately the operation allowed Amelia a degree of pain relief she had not experienced in years.

During the rest of 1924 and into 1925, Amelia seemed unable to decide on a career or course of study. She briefly returned to Columbia to take classes, and she worked in several jobs, but nothing seemed to fit. Although she missed aviation terribly, she knew that without a job, flying was impossible.

A Social Worker in Boston

In the fall of 1926, Amelia interviewed for a position as an entry-level social worker at Boston's Denison House. Despite

Denison House

One of the oldest settlement houses in the United States, Denison House was founded in 1892 by three college-educated women—Helen Cheever, Vida Scudder, and Emily Greene Balch—to serve a portion of Boston's immigrant population. Initially located in a neighborhood composed mainly of Syrian, Italian, Greek, and Chinese residents, the services provided by Denison House included sports and recreational programs for children, English language classes, dancing, and clubs for adults, as well as relief programs for the emergency distribution of necessities such as coal and milk. During the time Amelia Earhart lived at Denison, the settlement house consisted of a complex of five row houses (structures built side-by-side with adjoining walls). In addition to offices and rooms for residents, the facility also housed a library, clinic, and gymnasium and served as the center of many neighborhood activities.

In 1926, Amelia joined the staff at Boston's Denison House as a social worker.

her lack of experience, she got the job and went to work as the assistant to Marion Perkins, the director of the well-known **settlement house**. Amelia's enthusiasm for her new job was apparent to all. At last she had found something that truly interested her and gave her a sense of making a valuable contribution to the world around her.

. . . she knew that without a job, flying was impossible.

During Amelia's first year at Denison House, she oversaw the evening programs for immigrant men and women living in the area. Her duties rapidly expanded to include organizing games and outings for children, transporting people to and from medical appointments in her bright yellow car, and teaching classes about citizenship. Within a year, Amelia was a full-time resident employee, well-liked by the staff and area citizens alike.

By 1928, she had been appointed to the board of directors of Denison House as well as serving as the organization's secretary. Each position was quite an honor for a relatively new staff member. Many people with great social work expertise saw Amelia as a promising star with a bright future in this field. Those who knew Amelia well felt that the satisfaction she earned from her settlement work might have been enough for her had she not been involved with aviation. However, fate—in the form of a most unusual telephone call—stepped in.

CHAPTER 5

A Daring Adventure

Probably my greatest satisfaction was to indicate by example now and then, that women can sometimes do things themselves if given the chance.

Although Amelia found her career in social work tremendously rewarding, she did not give up her first love. Now that she had a regular income, Amelia could pursue her interest in aviation.

William Kinner, the designer of Amelia's beloved *Canary*, wrote from Los Angeles to see if she would be willing to help him set up an East Coast location for marketing his planes. In the course of investigating possible sites, Amelia met a young architect, Harold T. Dennison (no relation to the Denison House), who was planning to build an airport in the area; Amelia became an early investor. She also contacted another F.A.I.-licensed female pilot, Ruth Nichols, about forming an organization of women flyers.

Now that she had a regular income, Amelia could pursue her interest in aviation.

As a Boston resident and licensed F.A.I. pilot, Amelia joined the local chapter of the National Aeronautic Association. While attending the organization's monthly meetings, Amelia was not intimidated by being the only female in a sea of men. Quite the contrary—she spoke out and was viewed by her fellow members as competent,

In one of her first interviews, in 1927, Amelia urged women to try flying. The following year she promised, "when women are ready there will be opportunity for them in aviation."

intelligent, well-liked, and quite knowledgeable about fund-raising. Soon Amelia was elected vice president of the Boston chapter— becoming the NAA's first female officer. Finding her public voice, Amelia wrote an article about women and aviation for *The Bostonian*, a popular area magazine. In "When Women Go Aloft," Amelia stated her belief that "there is no door closed to ability, so when women are ready there will be opportunity for them in aviation."

A Monumental Aviation Achievement

Aviation was very much in the forefront of world news that year when, on May 21, 1927, Charles Lindbergh landed his plane, the *Spirit of St. Louis*, in Paris. After flying for thirty-three hours, he had become the first person to fly solo nonstop across the Atlantic. Stepping out of his aircraft, Lindbergh had stepped into the history books. Virtually overnight, flying and the aviation industry in general skyrocketed in popularity.

It was not surprising that a few days following the Lindbergh announcement, Amelia's name hit the area headlines when she flew over Boston distributing pamphlets about an upcoming benefit for Denison

"TAKE TO AIR," WOMAN FLIER URGES HER SEX

AMELIA EARHART

Miss Earhart Surprised That More Do Not Make Use of Planes

Miss Amelia Earhart, teacher, social worker, sportswoman and airplane pilot, paused in her duties at Denison House, 93 Tyler street, yesterday, long enough to express wonderment that other New England women do not take to the air for recreation.

"New England has some of the best yachtswomen and sportswomen in the world," she declared. "I am surprised that more New England women have not gone into flying as a sport. Why is it?"

Her interviewer, having a great fondness for flying, was unable to furnish an answer. There seemed to be none, other than the fact that New England's womenfolk have not yet become air conscious."

SHE IS ON DIRECTORATE OF DENNISON AIRCRAFT CORP.

Miss Earhart, who is a member of the flying staff and board of directors of the Dennison Aircraft Corporation, which on July 2 opens Boston's second

Charles Lindbergh (1902–1974)

Nicknamed the "Lone Eagle" and "Lucky Lindy" by the press, twenty-five-year-old Charles Augustus Lindbergh achieved worldwide fame when he became the first person to fly solo nonstop across the Atlantic on May 20–21, 1927. As he piloted his single-engine airplane, the *Spirit of St. Louis*, some 3,600 miles from New York to Paris in thirty-three and one-half hours, Lindbergh battled tiredness, fog, and icy conditions. His custom-built airplane had been designed to accommodate as much fuel as possible. In order to balance the weight of the engine and fuel tanks, the cockpit was located farther back in the plane. This unusual design meant the pilot could not see straight ahead unless he used a periscope or turned the plane to look out a side window.

Following Lindbergh's feat, it seemed nearly every well-known aviator—and some not-so-well-known—wanted to repeat it or best his record. In the next year, fifty-five individuals in eighteen planes attempted to cross the Atlantic—of those, only eight adventurers made it. Five of the unsuccessful flyers were women, and of those five, three died.

Ten days after his successful Atlantic solo flight, "Lucky Lindy" stands in front of his famous plane.

House. Although she had only been a passenger—a Harvard Flying Club member had flown while Amelia dropped the printed sheets—Amelia was the person mentioned in the papers: "Miss Amelia Earhart Flies in a Plane over Boston; Advertises Cedar Hill Carnival" read one.

An Irresistible Offer

One April afternoon in 1928, Amelia was called to the phone at Denison House. She did not like interruptions when she was working with the children, but took the call when she was told that it was urgent. On the telephone was Hilton H. Railey. Without wasting any time, he asked Amelia if she would be interested in doing something important for aviation—something that might be dangerous. At first Amelia thought the call was a joke or a request for her to do something illegal—like smuggling prohibited items across the United States border.

However, after asking Railey for references and confirming that they were legitimate, she agreed to meet him at his office that afternoon. "Curiosity," she later wrote, "is a great starter." Railey filled in as many of the details as he could about his proposal and ended with the all-important question, "How would you like to be the first woman to fly the Atlantic?" The chosen woman would be a passenger, not a pilot, on this historic flight, which Lindbergh had accomplished only a year before. Just a flicker in Amelia's clear gray eyes betrayed her interest as she calmly asked for more details. Without giving specific names, Railey told her as much of the story as he could.

Originally the flight was supposed to have been made by Amy Phipps Guest, a wealthy American married to a member of the British aristocracy. Convinced by her family that she should not make the dangerous crossing, Amy Guest decided to find a suitable replacement. She felt strongly that the first woman to fly across the Atlantic should be an American.

The task of finding the right candidate fell to Amy Guest's New York lawyer David T. Layman. More knowledgeable about legal issues than aviation, the attorney was relieved when he was contacted by publisher and promoter George Palmer Putnam, who offered Layman his assistance in finding the right woman passenger for the historic endeavor. G.P. (as he was known to many of his contemporaries) had learned about the supposedly-secret flight, and he sensed a big story.

Amy Guest was very clear about her requirements for this historic flight. In addition to being an American, the chosen woman had to be well-educated and well-spoken, with proper manners and an attractive appearance. G.P. assured Layman he would find just the right woman for the job. He started with the Boston contact—Hilton R. Railey—

"How would you like to be the first woman to fly the Atlantic?"

who had first supplied him with information about the flight itself. Railey, a newspaperman and publicist, then asked a friend who was a member of the Boston chapter of the NAA for suggestions. Railey was instructed to call Denison House and ask for Amelia. Railey felt that she clearly fit the bill. The fact that Amelia also happened to be a pilot herself was a major point in her favor. At the end of their appointment, Railey indicated to Amelia that she would be contacted again.

In May, after waiting for what seemed like an eternity, Amelia was called in for a second interview—this time in New York with David Layman, G.P., and Amy Guest's brother John Phipps. The decision was made a few days later—Amelia was the unanimous choice. No one else was even interviewed.

George Palmer Putnam (1887–1950)

Grandson of the noted publisher of the same name, George Palmer Putnam was born into an East Coast family of comfort and privilege. After a brief newspaper career in Oregon and military service during World War I, George returned to New York to head his family's publishing business, G.P. Putnam's Sons, following the unexpected death of his older brother during the 1918 flu epidemic. George's interest in exploration and adventure was mirrored in the books he published. These

included Charles Lindbergh's *We*, an account of his historic transatlantic solo flight, and several volumes by the polar explorer and aviator Admiral Richard E. Byrd. His marriage to the Crayola heiress Dorothy Binney produced two sons, but ended in a divorce in 1929.

Described by friends and foes as driven, overbearing, aggressive, and insensitive, George was a true promoter. Beginning in 1928, he used his considerable talents to successfully advance the career of aviator Amelia Earhart, whom he

Publisher, promoter, author, and explorer George Palmer Putnam eventually took on the full-time job of managing Amelia's busy career.

would later marry. After leaving his family's publishing company in the 1930s, George focused primarily on managing Amelia's career. Following her disappearance, he started his own publishing company in California and eventually served as an intelligence officer during World War II. George remarried twice more before dying of kidney failure on January 4, 1950.

Preparing for the Flight

Amy Guest made arrangements for a suitable plane and had it outfitted for the flight. Named the *Friendship* to honor British-American relations, the Fokker F-7 had originally been ordered by Admiral Richard E. Byrd for use in an upcoming expedition to the Antarctic, but Guest was able to persuade Byrd to part with the plane. Extra fuel tanks brought the three-motor plane's fuel capacity up to nearly nine hundred gallons—estimated to be enough for an Atlantic crossing. The *Friendship* was also outfitted with pontoons for water landings and painted a bright orange to make it easy to spot if it went down at sea. With a wingspan of seventy-two feet, the aircraft weighed more than five tons when fully loaded.

The rest of the *Friendship*'s crew was also put into place. The pilot/navigator, twenty-eight-year-old Wilmer "Bill" Stultz, had trained as a Navy flyer in Pensacola, Florida, and was an expert seaplane pilot. He also had extensive experience in meteorology and navigation. Louis "Slim" Gordon, a twenty-seven-year-old Texan who had been a chief mechanic at Maryland's Aberdeen Proving Grounds, knew aircraft engines inside and out.

Soaring across the Atlantic on the *Friendship*, Amelia earned instant fame. The tri-motor seaplane was painted bright orange for easy visibility.

Amelia had been told up front that Stultz and Gordon would be paid for the flight—Gordon, five thousand dollars, and Stultz, twenty thousand dollars. She would be paid nothing as she would be traveling only as a passenger—nothing more. Any money Amelia received in connection with the flight—such as the profits earned from the first-person newspaper account she was expected to write directly after the trip—were to be returned to help pay for the costs of the flight. However, there was no doubt that the flight—if successful—would bring Amelia great fame and likely great fortune as well. She also sensed, even then, the possibilities in aviation that this flight would open for women, and those possibilities—to Amelia—were invaluable.

Every attempt was made to keep preparations for the Atlantic crossing a secret. Those who saw the aircraft being serviced assumed it was still being fitted for Byrd's upcoming Antarctic expedition. Amelia stayed far away from the plane to avoid having reporters make any connection. During her wait for

She would be paid nothing as she would be traveling only as a passenger—nothing more.

the flight, Amelia continued to work at Denison House. She told only a few friends about her plans—among them were Marion Perkins and Sam Chapman.

To her mother and sister, she said not a word. She had asked Sam to tell them in person once she took off. Amelia also wrote a simple will—her possessions were minimal—as well as two notes ("popping-off letters" she called them) to be given to her parents if the flight failed. To her father she wrote, "Hooray for the last grand adventure! I wish I had won, but it was worthwhile anyway. You know that." To her mother, "My life has really been very happy, and I didn't mind contemplating its end in the midst of it."

Never delivered, but written to her father in case the *Friendship* went down, Amelia's "popping-off letter" expresses little regret. Before her successful crossing, some fifty individuals had failed in their transatlantic attempts.

Departure of the *Friendship*

Amelia's gear for the trip was very simple: a small knapsack containing a toothbrush, comb, hand cream, and two handkerchiefs, as well as a camera, binoculars, a copy of Byrd's volume *Skyward*, and a small logbook. Her clothes were those she would wear on board: a white silk blouse with a red necktie, brown riding britches, tall lace-up boots, a sweater, a helmet, goggles, a silk scarf, her precious leather coat, and a fur-lined flying suit.

After three false starts due to poor weather conditions, departure was finally set for June 3, 1928. Waking at 3:30 a.m., the flyers and their party breakfasted at an all-night restaurant before taking a tugboat out to the plane. G.P. was there to see them off, as well as Sam Chapman, Marion Perkins, and several others. After leaving the water at 6:31 a.m., the *Friendship* headed off into the rising sun.

CHAPTER 6

Flight of the *Friendship*

Adventure is worthwhile in itself.

On the first leg of the *Friendship's* historic journey, the flyers would head northward along the Atlantic coastline from Boston to Trepassey, Newfoundland, where they would briefly stop to pick up more fuel before crossing the Atlantic Ocean.

Once in the air, the crew encountered problems almost immediately. A faulty cabin door lock had been broken just before takeoff. The handle was tied to a gas can to keep the door closed, but the can wasn't heavy enough. Amelia saw the can begin to slide toward the slowly opening door and had to dive to save it—nearly throwing herself out of the plane in the process. After that, the door was tied more securely to a cabin brace.

Then, about halfway to Trepassey, the fog got so thick that it became necessary to backtrack for fifty miles and land in Halifax, Nova Scotia, before heading on to Trepassey the next day. At first they anticipated only a brief stopover in Trepassey to gather weather data, refuel the plane, and rest overnight, but the crew's stay in the tiny town stretched on . . . and on.

The Long Wait

At first the delay seemed like an advantage. The oil tank had been leaking and Slim Gordon used the opportunity to repair it with cement and tape. However, trying to load gasoline became a grueling chore that gale-force winds soon made impossible. In addition, the heavy weight of the plane combined with the narrow shape and high hills of Trepassey Harbor meant they could only take off in a southwesterly direction and only in good weather. Without the right conditions, the flyers were effectively trapped.

In the meantime, once the flyers had left Boston the news broke. Telegrams began pouring into Trepassey, and reporters soon followed. Unfortunately, Sam Chapman had not been able to reach Amy and Muriel Earhart before they read about the flight in the newspaper. Knowing of her family's probable distress, Amelia telegraphed her mother as soon as possible from Newfoundland. Amy's response was loving and supportive: "WE ARE NOT WORRYING WISH I WERE WITH YOU GOOD LUCK AND CHEERIO LOVE MOTHER."

While G.P. remained at his post in New York, carefully monitoring the weather bureau's reports, Hilton Railey had already

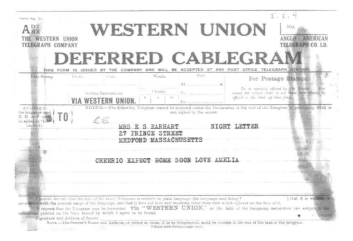

Telegraphing her mother once the *Friendship* crew was poised for takeoff in Newfoundland, Amelia purposefully kept her message upbeat.

sailed for Europe. If the three flyers made a successful crossing, he would be in charge of coordinating publicity on that end.

The three aviators spent endless hours playing cards, reading, seeing what little there was to see in the area, and simply waiting. Despite their repeated attempts, they had not been able to get out of Trepassey Harbor. Personal cleanliness also became a bit of an issue, but Amelia seemed to take it in stride. When sent a telegram by G.P. expressing some concern about her limited wardrobe, she teasingly replied: "THANKS FATHERLY TELEGRAM NO WASHING NECESSARY SOCKS UNDERWEAR WORN-OUT SHIRT LOST TO SLIM [GORDON] AT RUMMY CHEERIO A.E."

The news that other flyers were readying their planes to attempt an Atlantic crossing did not improve matters. But a more serious problem arose with Bill Stultz, who had begun to drink excessively. Perhaps reminded of her father's battle with alcoholism, Amelia was at first uncertain what to do. She had the authority to decide whether to replace Bill and knew G.P. had a backup pilot on call if needed. However, despite his current condition, Bill—when he was sober—was the better pilot, and Amelia knew that firing him would end his career as an aviator.

Despite their repeated attempts, they had not been able to get out of Trepassey Harbor.

At 11 p.m. on June 16, after spending nearly two nerve-racking weeks in Trepassey, Amelia received word from G.P. that favorable weather conditions seemed to be in store for the crew. Dr. James Kimball, chief meteorologist of the New York Weather Bureau, had given the flight a green light. Her decision was made for her—Amelia would stick with Bill Stultz. G.P. later called it "either the bravest or the silliest act of her whole career."

Doc Kimball (1874–1943)

Dr. James H. Kimball served as chief meteorologist of the New York Weather Bureau during the early years of transatlantic air travel. Affectionately referred to as "Doc" by pioneering aviators of the day, Kimball—who had never flown himself—used reports telegraphed from ships at sea and land stations in the U.S., Canada, Bermuda, Greenland, England, and the Arctic to devise weather forecast charts that were invaluable to early flyers. Doc was relied upon for data and weather predictions by famous pilots such as Charles Lindbergh, Admiral Richard E. Byrd, and Amelia Earhart, who once noted, "we shoved off only when he said go."

From his office atop the Whitehall Building in lower Manhattan, Doc sometimes worked throughout the night to gather details affecting North Atlantic travel. Visibility, temperature, barometric pressure, wind speed and direction, and local weather conditions were all factors that went into the compilation of his reports.

At a dinner in 1931, held in Doc's honor, one reporter covering the event wrote that Doc was "largely responsible for the success of every oceanic flight starting from the Atlantic coast."

Famous flyers gather to honor "Doc" Kimball (seated far left). Amelia is seated second from the left and Charles Lindbergh stands behind her.

Finally Getting Underway

The next morning, June 17, Amelia and Slim Gordon guided the severely hungover pilot out to the *Friendship*. It was now or never. Hopefully instinct would take over once Bill Stultz was in the air.

To ensure success, the decision was made to lighten the plane's load as much as possible. Gone were their life jackets, rubber life raft, and some two hundred gallons of gasoline. Originally, the flyers had planned to land in Southampton, England; now they just hoped to safely reach the Irish coast. With limited fuel, their margin for error was slim.

After so many false starts, few were on hand to watch what they assumed was yet another unsuccessful attempt by the *Friendship* to depart. Amazingly, the plane finally lifted into the air at 12:21 p.m. local time. The takeoff had lasted an agonizing three minutes as the aircraft plowed heavily along, its wing-mounted engines sputtering from sprays of saltwater. After a few minutes in flight, the *Friendship* made one last, low pass over Trepassey before heading northeast to the Atlantic. The local telegraph operator sent a prearranged coded message to G.P. signaling their departure: "VIOLET CHEERIO AMELIA." Finally, they were on their way.

A Difficult Flight

Only about an hour off Newfoundland, the *Friendship* ran into a storm system. Poor visibility and bad weather continued for most of the flight, and Bill Stultz's skills as a pilot were put to the test. It quickly became apparent that Amelia, who had hoped to do some piloting of the plane, would simply remain a passenger on this journey across the Atlantic. At this point in her aviation career she had no experience "flying blind" (relying almost solely on instruments to determine a plane's position in the air).

Because of its proximity to Europe, Trepassey, Newfoundland, was an ideal departure point for pilots flying across the Atlantic. As shown in this official photo taken about a decade before the *Friendship* flight, Trepassey Harbor also served as a testing site for the U.S. Navy's first flying boats.

Fortunately, the aircraft's northerly course meant long periods of daylight. The sun did not fully set until about 10 p.m. and rose at about 3 a.m. Despite the light, the cabin remained bitterly cold throughout the flight, and all three flyers appreciated the warmth of their fur-lined flying suits. Although they had brought some coffee and sandwiches on board, not much was eaten.

Amelia wrote diligently in the flight log, recording her impressions: "The clouds look like icebergs in the distance. . . . Darkness complete. Stultz sits alone, every muscle and nerve alert. Gordon sleeps. There are many hours to go." All through the long night, people on both sides of the Atlantic worried and wondered about the fate of the three flyers.

Running Low on Fuel

Morning brought the most tense hours. Fuel was low. The radio had stopped operating. One motor was coughing and sputtering. Time was running out. They should have spotted the

Irish coast by now. At about 10:30 a.m. local time, the three flyers glimpsed a large ocean liner through a break in the clouds. Although they didn't know it at the time, this was the SS *America*.

Initially cheered by the sight, the *Friendship* crew was dismayed to realize the big ship was traveling on a path perpendicular to theirs. If they were on course, the liner should have been traveling parallel to them in the shipping lanes that headed to and from the Irish coast. Were they lost? What the flyers didn't realize was that they had already flown over Ireland. In the cloudy conditions, they had been

Fuel was low. The radio had stopped operating. One motor was coughing and sputtering.

unable to see land. Instead, they were on the other side, flying across the Irish Sea, heading towards Wales.

Amelia made two unsuccessful attempts to drop a message asking their position. She tossed bagged notes weighted with oranges from the plane's bottom hatchway, hoping to hit the SS *America*'s deck, but they landed in the water instead. Fearful of wasting more valuable fuel by attempting to communicate with the ship, Stultz made the decision to keep their present course and continue onward.

Landing in Wales

Soon a dark shape loomed out of the fog. Although they had been fooled earlier by clouds that looked like land, this form remained and grew larger. A rocky coastline appeared. "*It was land!*" Amelia recalled after the flight. "I think Slim yelled. I know [his] sandwich went flying out the window. Bill permitted himself a smile." Knowing they were dangerously low on fuel, Stultz did not want to venture very far inland because the pontoon-equipped *Friendship* could only land on water.

Flying along the coast, he spotted a little bay near a village. As the plane touched down, Amelia wrote in her logbook, "20 hrs. 40 min. out of Trepassey. *Friendship* down safely in harbor of _____." The blank would be filled in once the flyers found out where they were. Taxiing over to a buoy located about one-half mile from shore, the two men quickly tied the plane down to keep it from drifting. They had made it. They had crossed the Atlantic!

They were just offshore from the little mining town of Burry Port, Wales, which seemed to be the only place in the western world that had not heard about the *Friendship*'s extraordinary attempt. Despite hand signals and yells, nothing the flyers could do seemed to attract anyone's attention. Three men working on

Awaiting transport to land, Amelia stands on one of the *Friendship*'s pontoons. Although locals gathered on shore, an hour passed before harbor police rowed out to investigate the new arrivals.

a railroad track glanced up when the plane arrived, but then turned their backs, continuing with their task at hand.

Eventually a small crowd gathered on the shoreline, but no attempt was made to reach the flyers. Amelia waved a white towel out the open cockpit window (white being the international signal for distress), hoping to get a response. One gentleman on shore waved back enthusiastically, but that was all. Finally, after about an hour of waiting, the harbor policeman rowed out and took Bill Stultz back to shore where he could call Hilton Railey, who was waiting in Southampton.

Railey immediately chartered a seaplane and headed to Burry Port. His first glimpse of Amelia was of her sitting Indian-style in the cockpit doorway—cool and composed. Several more hours

Although Amelia later compared her presence on the *Friendship* to a "sack of potatoes," her smile betrays the excitement she obviously felt upon successfully crossing the Atlantic as one of the crew.

Still wearing her fur-lined flying suit, Amelia signs autographs for enthusiastic spectators on the Welsh shoreline.

passed before the *Friendship* was tied to a mooring and all three flyers were ashore. By then the weather had worsened, and the decision was made to postpone the flight on to Southampton until morning.

Once word of the plane's arrival reached the airwaves, some ten thousand Welsh citizens gathered to greet the three adventurers, with only a handful of clearly overwhelmed policemen to manage the crowd. "In the enthusiasm of their greeting," recalled Amelia, "those hospitable people nearly tore our clothes off." It was 10 p.m. before Amelia, Bill, and Slim were finally able to sit down to dinner. But the greetings of the people in Wales would barely prepare the flyers for what awaited them the next day.

CHAPTER 7

Admired and Adored

After the pleasant accident of being the first woman to cross the Atlantic by air, I was launched into a life full of interest.

With a light load and just fifty gallons of fuel on board, the *Friendship* easily lifted off from the Burry Port harbor the next morning. In addition to the three flyers, the plane also carried Hilton Railey and a reporter from the *New York Times*.

At last Amelia was able to pilot the plane for a brief period before Bill Stultz returned to the controls for the Southampton landing. The harbor was so jam-packed with ships of all sizes that the *Friendship* had to circle several times before the green lights of a signal gun indicated

Landing in the harbor at Southampton, England, the morning after their successful Atlantic flight, the *Friendship* and its crew taxis toward waiting well-wishers.

From left to right, Amy Phipps Guest, Lou Gordon, Amelia, Bill Stultz, and the mayor of Southampton, Mrs. Foster Welch, pose for the press on the Southampton dock.

where it should land. Tugboat whistles, wailing sirens, booming foghorns, and the cheers of the crowd filled the air as the plane's pontoons touched down.

The crew and the passengers were transferred to a **launch**, which carried them to shore. There to greet them was Amy Phipps Guest, Amelia's **patron** and sponsor. Next, the three flyers were officially greeted dockside by Mrs. Foster Welch, the mayor of Southampton. Amelia was pleased to see a woman mayor. While British bobbies (policemen) held back the crowds of well-wishers, Amelia climbed into a yellow Rolls-Royce for the drive into London.

Just Baggage ... For Now

The flyers—especially Amelia—were amazed by the reception they received. Despite the newsworthiness of being the first woman to fly across the Atlantic, Amelia did not feel she deserved any special recognition. After all, it was Bill Stultz and Slim Gordon who had done the work. "I was just baggage," she had told Hilton Railey, "like a sack of potatoes." But people were fascinated by the attractive young woman. U.S. President Calvin Coolidge cabled Amelia directly, "I WISH TO EXPRESS TO YOU, THE FIRST WOMAN SUCCESSFULLY TO SPAN THE NORTH ATLANTIC BY

Fashionably dressed in one of several new outfits she purchased upon arrival, Amelia accompanies Amy Guest and her sons to a racecourse outside London.

AIR, THE GREAT ADMIRATION OF MYSELF AND THE PEOPLE OF THE UNITED STATES FOR YOUR SPLENDID FLIGHT." Amelia, in her reply, was quick to assert, "SUCCESS ENTIRELY DUE GREAT SKILL OF MR. STULTZ."

Throughout the flyers' stay in London, which expanded gradually from the originally-scheduled three days to ten, Amelia insisted she was merely a passenger on the flight and little-deserving of so much attention. "Maybe some day," she said, "I'll try it alone."

Since Amelia had brought no wardrobe other than the clothes on her back—now very worn after the unexpected length of her stay in Newfoundland—Amy Guest made arrangements for her to acquire clothing suitable for the many social events scheduled. As she met various dignitaries, Amelia remained gracious, poised, and well-spoken.

Home in America

While heading home on the U.S. steamship the *President Roosevelt*, which departed on June 28, the three flyers were at last able to catch up on some rest. Before they reached American shores, the three received word from G.P. that they had already been invited to special welcoming ceremonies in thirty-two U.S.

Bill Stultz and Lou Gordon flank Amelia as they wave to record-sized crowds outside New York's City Hall on July 6, 1928.

cities. On July 6, they arrived in New York Harbor to another incredible greeting. Fireboats shot streams of water up in the air as the mayor's barge came out to meet their ship.

After a **ticker-tape** parade through town in an open car, the flyers arrived at City Hall for a reception. Amelia was dubbed "Lady Lindy" by some members of the press. The next day she was back in Boston—where her mother and sister waited at the airport—for yet another joyous welcome. Everywhere she went, people wanted to catch a glimpse of the attractive young pilot. Along the Boston parade route, Amelia glimpsed children from Denison House—where she planned to resume her career as a social worker once the celebrations were over. After Boston, the three flyers headed by train to Chicago and many other stops for more festivities. Finally, the crew of the *Friendship* returned to New York.

Almost immediately, Amelia moved into the Putnams' home in Rye, New York, to write a book about the flight for G.P.'s publishing house. Finished on August 25, the volume hit bookstores by September 10. Dedicated to Amelia's hostess, G.P.'s wife, Dorothy, *20 Hrs. 40 Min., Our Flight in the* Friendship was an instant hit. Soon Amelia realized it was time to make some serious

Lady Lindy

Despite Amelia's claim that she had "the kind of face that looks like everybody," it was to Charles Lindbergh that she was most often compared. Jake Coolidge, a newsreel photographer, is credited with creating the "Lady Lindy" illusion through a clever combination of camera angles, poses, and aviator garb. While the nickname first surfaced after her initial Atlantic crossing aboard the *Friendship*, it stuck with Amelia throughout much of her career—despite the fact that she found it somewhat annoying and embarrassing. To Lindbergh's wife, Anne, she wrote, "I have never apologized so widely and so consistently for anything in my life." Yet after meeting Amelia in 1930, even Mrs. Lindbergh noticed a resemblance between the two flyers—perhaps not so much in looks, but definitely in temperament.

Many felt Lindbergh and Earhart resembled each other. Some thought Amelia looked like Lindbergh's double.

decisions about her career in social work, her relationship with Sam Chapman, and her future. But for the time being, more than anything else, she wanted to *fly*.

Across the Country and Back

When Amelia was in England, she had purchased a light plane called an Avro Avian. The previous owner, Lady Mary Heath, had been the first British woman to obtain a transport pilot's license (the highest rating available to civilian pilots). The little plane's **fuselage** was adorned with medals and plaques from Lady Heath's travels. To it, she added another: "To Amelia Earhart from Mary Heath. Always think with your stick forward."

Exactly where Amelia, with her limited income as a social worker, obtained the $3,200 (the equivalent of $34,000 today) to purchase the plane is unknown. Some biographers believe G.P. may have loaned her the money, banking on the fame Amelia was sure to attain once she returned to the United States. In any event, the plane was crated and shipped back to America— arriving at about the same time that Amelia finished writing her book. The timing was perfect—she was ready to set some records of her own.

Amelia returned from the *Friendship* crossing with a new plane, an Avro Avian. Here bystanders surround Amelia as she sits in the Avian's cockpit not long after the aircraft's arrival in the U.S.

Without making any sort of formal announcement, Amelia took off from New York on August 31, 1928. Her intention was to finally take the cross-country plane trip she had dreamed about when she left California in 1924. But this time she would be traveling in the opposite direction. Calling it a vacation flight, Amelia took G.P. along as her passenger for part of the trip.

The timing was perfect— she was ready to set some records of her own.

Trouble appeared at Amelia's first stopover at a farm field outside Pittsburgh. When rolling to a stop after an uneventful landing, the plane hit a shallow ditch and nearly flipped over. The pilot and passenger were fine, but the aircraft needed some serious repairs—including a new propeller and new landing gear. Parts were hard to come by for the European-made plane, but somehow G.P. managed to locate them and repairs were completed within forty-eight hours. After dropping G.P. off in Dayton, Ohio, Amelia continued across the country—her first long-distance solo flight.

Delays for repairs, local weather and wind conditions, and navigation errors extended the trip to nearly two weeks. As she traveled westward, Amelia stayed with both friends and strangers. When she reached Los Angeles, there was time for a visit with her father, who was now remarried. Taking a more northerly route on her return trip, Amelia was back in New York in mid-October. There she stepped into the record books as the first woman pilot to make a solo flight across the country and back.

By then Amelia had had the time to make some serious decisions about her life. Despite her love of social work, she would not be returning to Denison House. Aviation was her future. In November she broke things off with Sam Chapman.

Sam never got married, and he remained friends with Amelia for the rest of her life.

Image Appeal

With the twin successes of *20 Hrs. 40 Min.* and her round-trip coast-to-coast flight, Amelia was booked by G.P. on a series of lecture tours around the country. Flying whenever she could in order to publicize both aviation and women as pilots, Amelia sometimes traveled to as many as thirty different locations in a single month. Around this same time, *McCall's* magazine offered her a job as their aviation editor. Amelia also agreed to make her first product endorsement. It almost turned out to be her last.

In order to help raise funds needed for Admiral Richard E. Byrd's upcoming expedition to the Antarctic, Amelia agreed to lend her name—and image—to an advertisement for Lucky Strike cigarettes. Although she never smoked (or drank alcohol), she did the ad and donated the $1,500 fee she was paid to Byrd's endeavor.

Unfortunately, her generosity backfired. In 1929, the concept of a woman advertising cigarettes was very daring—too daring, it appeared, for *McCall's*, who took back their job offer. Fortunately for

Though not a smoker herself, Amelia agreed to let Lucky Strike cigarettes use her image in an ad to raise funds for Admiral Byrd's Antarctic expedition. Her gesture backfired, costing her a job.

Amelia, *Cosmopolitan* magazine had no such concerns, and she became their aviation editor instead. Articles such as "Why Are Women Afraid to Fly?" and "Try Flying Yourself!" carried Amelia's

Selling the Image

Flying was—and is—an expensive endeavor. Despite Amelia's many achievements and great popularity, the financing of her aviation career was a constant challenge. In addition to the income she earned from public speaking, Amelia also allowed her name to be used for the promotion of various products. At one time or another, these included movie cameras, stationery, watches, automobiles, engine oil, chewing gum, and a variety of aviation products. In 1933, a line of lightweight luggage especially designed for air travel bore her name. It was still sold long after her death. Even today, Amelia's image appears in advertisements—such as recent promotions for Gap™ clothing (1993) and Apple™ computers (2002).

In addition to product endorsements, Amelia also made various public appearances at special events. These included new aircraft and automobile christenings and deep-sea diving and parachute jump demonstrations. Amelia even had her eyes examined by the Better Vision Institute in 1931 atop New York's newly-opened Empire State Building.

"Flying with me is a business. Of course I make money. I have to or I couldn't fly," Amelia told reporters in a 1935 interview. "I've got to be self-supporting or I couldn't stay in the business."

Endorsements helped pay for Amelia's costly flying expenses. Here she demonstrates a training device for parachute jumps.

byline. The constant theme running through her articles was how safe flying really was. She encouraged all women—wives, mothers, and daughters—to take to the air. In one article, Amelia wrote about her own mother, for whom flying had become so routine that she now usually brought along a novel to read while her daughter was piloting them around the country.

Although Amelia still appeared in many photos dressed in her flight gear, with G.P.'s influence the image of her as a beautiful and fashionable woman began to evolve. Her slender figure, freckled nose, short hair, and long-legged stride seemed to personify style and grace. She was photographed for magazine articles in riding clothes, ball gowns, flowing skirts, and—more often than not—pants.

. . . with G.P.'s influence, the image of her as a beautiful and fashionable woman began to evolve.

Amelia was very self-conscious about her ankles, which she felt were thick and unattractive. Pants were the perfect solution, and the ones she wore were usually beautifully tailored. A woman in pants was still not that common a sight, but Amelia had the figure to wear them, and the public noticed.

She also had lovely hands. Many who met her were surprised by their beauty—especially for hands that tinkered with engines and worked with airplanes. "The tapering loveliness of her hands was almost unbelievable," G.P. once wrote, "found in one who did the things she did." Hats, though, were out. "Your hats!" G.P. had written in a letter to Amelia, "They are a public menace. You should do something about them when you must wear them at all!" Following G.P.'s pointed assessment, Amelia almost never appeared wearing a hat again—and her short, windblown curls became her trademark.

CHAPTER 8

Marriage and More

I knew I had found the one person who could put up with me.

The first Women's Transcontinental Air Derby was scheduled to begin in August of 1929, in Santa Monica, California, and end in Cleveland, Ohio. That spring Amelia had begun her search for a newer, more powerful airplane. By the end of July, she had sold her Avian and purchased a Lockheed Vega. The plane she selected could carry five passengers and had been used as a demonstration aircraft on the East Coast.

With fewer than three weeks to go before the start of the race, Amelia and another pilot took turns flying the plane out to Burbank, California, so Lockheed mechanics could fine-tune it before the air derby. A company test pilot named Wiley Post (who would later achieve great fame as the first aviator to fly solo around the world) took Amelia's plane up for a trial flight.

In a publicity shot for her entrance in the first Transcontinental Women's Air Derby, held in 1929, Amelia stands in the cockpit of her new Lockheed Vega.

When he returned he announced that he thought the Lockheed aircraft was in terrible shape.

Conscious of Amelia's growing fame and the importance of the upcoming race, Lockheed offered Amelia a brand-new plane in trade for hers. Amelia was big news in the pages of the media, and Lockheed knew the resulting publicity from this gesture would bring good press coverage for the company as well. This Vega could also carry five passengers and boasted a 220-horsepower engine. While it was wonderful to have a brand-new aircraft, the switch left Amelia with very little time to get used to her new plane before the start of the derby.

Many male reporters referred to the race as the "Powder Puff Derby" and called its entrants "Ladybirds" or "Sweethearts of the Air." Amelia later commented dryly that "We are still trying to get ourselves called just 'pilots.'" Regardless, the Women's Air Derby was a serious event. The winner would receive a prize of $2,500 (which is nearly $30,000 today).

The Women's Air Derby

In order to be eligible to enter the race, women had to be licensed pilots and have a minimum of one hundred hours of flying experience. On the afternoon of August 18, 1929, nineteen women and their planes ended up on the starting line. With few established airfields along the way, these pilots would be flying solo across the country under extremely challenging conditions. All flyers were required to carry a three-day supply of food and one gallon of water in case they were forced down by engine trouble in a remote area.

Overnight stops were prearranged, and no night flying was permitted. Departures were scheduled as last-in-first-out, meaning that the last flyer to arrive each evening was allowed to take off

Though dubbed the "Powder Puff Derby" by some members of the press, the race was serious business. On August 18, 1929, participants and their planes stand ready for the starting signal.

first the next morning. Pilots had eight days to fly the 2,350 miles from Santa Monica to Cleveland. Cash prizes would be awarded for winning various legs of the race, and the combined time for completion of all sections of the race would determine the overall winner.

Taking off at one-minute intervals, the women pilots flew off toward the first overnight stop located less than one hundred miles away in San Bernardino, California. From then on, the flyers rose at dawn; each long day of flying became a grueling test of endurance. In Columbus, Ohio, the last stop before Cleveland, Amelia and another pilot, Ruth Nichols, were in the lead. Just as Ruth took off, her plane's wing hit a tractor parked at the end of the runway. Amelia, who was supposed to be the next pilot to take off, cut her engine and ran over to check on her friend and

Pilots had eight days to fly the 2,350 miles from Santa Monica to Cleveland.

competitor. Despite her wrecked aircraft, Ruth Nichols was fine, but the delay in departure may have cost Amelia the win. She ended up in third place.

In all, sixteen pilots crossed the finish line in Cleveland. Despite one fatality, caused when a pilot had attempted to parachute out of her plane as it was diving at a low altitude, the race was considered a triumph for women's aviation. It was, Amelia later noted, "a chance to play the game as men play it, by rules established for them as flyers, not as women."

A Women's Aviation Organization

Just a few weeks after the success of the first Women's Air Derby, four pilots—Neva Paris, Frances Harrell, Margery Brown, and Fay Gillis—sent out a letter to the 117 licensed female pilots in the U.S., inviting them to join an aviation organization for women. It was an idea that Amelia had endorsed since before her flight aboard the *Friendship*.

That November, a group of women pilots met at Long Island's Curtiss Field. Their basic goal was "to provide a close relationship among women pilots and to unite them in any movement that may be for their benefit or for that of aviation in general." The organization—eventually named the Ninety-Nines—is still going strong today.

More Flying Records

Amelia spent the last weeks of 1929 staying with friends in California. She also visited her father and his wife, who lived outside Los Angeles. Frail and ill, Edwin Earhart was once again in financial trouble. Unable to work steadily due to his health, he worried about being able to make the mortgage payments on his home—a simple cabin surrounded by five acres of land. Amelia

The Ninety-Nines

Founded on November 2, 1929, primarily to advance the role of women in aviation, one of the organization's first tasks was to choose a name. After suggestions such as the Lady Birds, the Cloud Chasers, and the Homing Pigeons were considered and discarded, it was Amelia Earhart who proposed that the group be named after the number of charter members who had joined. Ninety-nine women had joined during the initial registration period, and the "Ninety-Nines" was born. The only requirement for membership was—and still is—an up-to-date pilot's license. While early meetings were somewhat informal, by 1932 the organization became more structured, and Amelia was elected its first president.

Today more than 5,500 women pilots from around the world belong to the Ninety-Nines. Although the majority of its members live in the U.S., more than thirty other countries are also represented. In addition to sponsoring educational and aviation safety programs, the Ninety-Nines maintain and coordinate an international air marking program that provides navigation aids and identification markers for pilots in flight.

Each year the group's Amelia Earhart Memorial Scholarship is awarded to qualified members for training or advanced study in specialized fields of aviation. The Ninety-Nines' Oklahoma City headquarters houses invaluable documents, oral histories, video and film collections, and other artifacts tracing the history of women in flight.

Members of the Ninety-Nines gather in 1935 to honor their famous comrade Amelia Earhart. Amelia suggested the aviation organization's name based on the number of its original members.

made arrangements to pay off the $2,000 balance her father owed, therefore providing him with some security for the future. She feared he did not have much longer to live, and she was correct. The following September, just hours after a last visit with Amelia, Edwin Earhart died at the age of sixty-three. Amelia wired her sister Muriel, "DAD'S LAST BIG CASE SETTLED OUT OF COURT, PEACEFULLY AND WITHOUT PAIN."

Amelia had spent the months before her father's death traveling the lecture circuit, speaking to audiences across the country. In March she had traded in her plane for a larger and more powerful model. This state-of-the-art Lockheed Vega, though also a five-passenger aircraft, had a bigger, 425-horsepower engine.

In April, she went on a one-month speaking tour throughout the Midwest—twenty-five appearances in thirty-one days. In May, she spoke to 250 female students at Barnard College. "There is no reason," she proclaimed, "why a woman can't hold any position in aviation providing she can overcome prejudices and show ability."

She feared he did not have much longer to live, and she was correct.

With all the hours of flight experience she had accumulated by May of 1930, Amelia was able to obtain her aviation commercial transport license, confirming her status as a professional pilot. She was only one of a handful of women to have achieved this. July found Amelia in Detroit where she set the women's world flying speed record of 181.18 miles per hour on a 1.86-mile (3-kilometer) course.

More Than a Business Partner

By now G.P. was serving as Amelia's manager, publicist, editor, advisor, wardrobe consultant, and near-constant companion.

Rumors began to circulate within the aviation community that their relationship was more than just business. When the news broke late in 1929 that G.P. and his wife had ended their marriage of nearly twenty years, both he and Amelia were bombarded with questions by reporters. While G.P. may have had other ideas, Amelia was not interested in a husband. Memories of her parents' troubled relationship may have influenced Amelia's feelings, but, more importantly, she valued her independence too much to consider marrying anyone.

As 1930 passed slowly by, G.P. began to speak more and more seriously of marriage. Biographers disagree as to the number of proposals he made to Amelia—some report as few as two or as many as six. G.P. himself later recalled that he had been turned down on at least two occasions. At Lockheed's Burbank facility later that fall, as Amelia waited for her plane's engines to warm up, G.P. proposed once more. Just before she climbed aboard her plane for takeoff, Amelia casually patted his arm and said yes.

G.P. applied for a marriage license almost immediately, but

Although concerned about the limitations marriage might place on her career, Amelia wed manager George Palmer Putnam on February 7, 1931.

Amelia was still unsure and would not discuss the couple's plans with reporters. Despite his background as a publicist, G.P. honored Amelia's wish that all details be kept from the press until the marriage had taken place. Amelia wore a simple brown suit to the five-minute ceremony on February 7, 1931, and almost immediately removed the thin platinum wedding band from her finger. In their joint announcement to the press, it was noted that the bride would retain her maiden name—Amelia Earhart— professionally.

Amelia was so resistant to the idea of a traditional marriage that she spent much of the night before the ceremony writing a letter to her husband-to-be, outlining her feelings about their future relationship. When judged by the standards of the day, it is almost brutally frank. "You must know again my reluctance to marry . . . I feel the move just now as foolish as anything I could do. I know there may be compensations, but have no heart to look ahead. . . . I must exact a cruel promise . . . [that] you will let me go in a year if we find no happiness together. I will try to do my best in every way." She was back at work the Monday following her marriage to G.P.

As 1930 passed slowly by, G.P. began to speak more and more seriously of marriage.

Many have wondered why Amelia and G.P. got married at all. Was it simply a marriage of convenience between a famous figure and her manager? Did their relationship evolve from one of mutual respect and companionship into something more? Perhaps above all else, Amelia valued her privacy, so there are no pages left from a diary or journal that explain her inner feelings. But Amelia always chose the path that she believed followed the truest course. No matter what had led her to this marriage, it would not stand in the way of her hopes and plans for the future.

CHAPTER 9

Atlantic Solo

I chose to fly the Atlantic because I wanted to.

Back on December 14, 1930, Amelia had become the first woman to fly an autogiro—an unusual aircraft that combined features of both the airplane and the helicopter. Writing of the experience later in her book *The Fun of It*, Amelia commented that she wasn't sure "whether I flew it or it flew me." On April 8, 1931, in Willow Grove, Pennsylvania, Amelia set a new altitude record of 18,415 feet in an autogiro, a record that would stand for years.

She was intrigued by the new "round-wing" aircraft and decided she wanted one of her own. Amelia also began to make plans to be the first autogiro pilot to fly across the country. G.P. made arrangements with the Beech-Nut company to sponsor the trip. In exchange, Amelia agreed to have the company's name appear in large letters on the side

Amelia pilots her autogiro over the Pennsylvania countryside during her 1931 cross-country flight. Amelia became the first person to fly across the U.S. and back in the new aircraft.

Autogiros

A forerunner of the modern helicopter, the autogiro was first developed by Juan de la Cierva, a Spanish aeronautical engineer, and made its first successful flight in 1923. Where a helicopter can rise vertically for takeoff, the autogiro had to taxi like an airplane, though for a shorter distance. The forward **airspeed**—instead of the engine—would then turn its rotor (four large blades mounted on a mast). Short, broad wings helped to provide stability and control during flight. Despite its ability to fly at very slow speeds and make vertical landings, the autogiro was not a commercial success. Plagued by technical problems and numerous accidents, few were in use by the onset of World War II. But the lessons learned from the autogiro's design helped the aviation industry's development of future rotary wing aircraft.

Juan de la Cierva's autogiro completes a successful test flight in London.

of her aircraft. Taking off from Newark, New Jersey, on May 29, Amelia carried aboard about a hundred pounds of tools and spare parts as well as a mechanic. It seemed wiser to bring everything on the trip rather than hope to find the right parts or tools for these experimental engines along the way.

Unfortunately, Amelia was beaten to the West Coast by another autogiro pilot who had landed safely just a week earlier. Amelia then made the return trip—arriving back in Newark on June 22—as the first pilot to have successfully flown an autogiro across the country *and back*. In all, she had traveled some eleven thousand miles and logged one hundred fifty hours in the air. The August issue of *Cosmopolitan* featured her article entitled "Your Next Garage May House an Autogiro."

Despite her willingness to publicize this new aircraft's appeal, Amelia found she really preferred airplanes. The experimental autogiros were too slow, too difficult to maintain, and required too many fuel stops.

Challenge of an Atlantic Flight

By this time, news agencies were reporting on several women pilots who were hoping to be the first to fly solo across the Atlantic. One pilot was Ruth Nichols, who had also flown in the first Women's Air Derby. While Amelia outwardly denied any interest in making the same trip, she was secretly formulating her plans. Although G.P. knew this was something Amelia had thought about doing since she traveled as "baggage" on the *Friendship* flight, he still wrote later that he felt a "clutch at the heart" when she began to seriously discuss the possibility.

While Amelia outwardly denied any interest in making the same trip, she was secretly formulating her plans.

That fall, Amelia also took time to work on another book. *The Fun of It: Random Records of My Own Flying and of Women in Aviation* offered stories of her childhood and piloting experiences intermixed with details about flying in general, some aviation history, and advice to parents of prospective flyers (such as "don't issue **edicts** against flying until you know something about it from experience").

Maintaining her usual calm and cool appearance for the press, Amelia, along with G.P., quietly made arrangements to meet with

Amelia's image graces an early edition of her popular 1932 autobiography, which contained stories of her own life as well as details about other famous women flyers.

Bernt Balchen, a well-known Norwegian flyer with excellent navigation and engineering experience, who had participated in expeditions to both the North and South Poles.

Amelia Earhart
THE FUN OF IT

Secret Preparations

It was agreed that Balchen would serve as Amelia's technical advisor for her proposed Atlantic solo flight. However, to create a diversion, Amelia arranged to supposedly loan her Lockheed Vega to Balchen for an upcoming South Pole flight that he was planning. With the plane in Balchen's hands at New Jersey's Teterboro Airport, arrangements could then be made for the modifications that would be necessary for an Atlantic crossing.

One of the most important changes that needed to be made was to increase the plane's fuel capacity. The two original wing tanks—which together carried about 100 gallons—were supplemented by eight more tanks that could carry an additional 420 gallons of fuel. These tanks—along with a new 500-horsepower supercharged engine—gave Amelia's plane a cruising range of 3,200 miles. This was more than enough fuel to reach Paris, her intended destination, which was about 2,640 miles from her point of departure.

Additional instruments were also installed—these included two new compasses, a drift indicator and a directional gyro (both would help Amelia keep on course), and new ailerons (the

Amelia's advisor for her Atlantic solo flight, Norwegian pilot Bernt Balchen, appears in this 1929 photo—the same year he became the first person to fly over the South Pole.

movable parts at the back of each wing that allow the plane to roll left or right). Once the aircraft was fully outfitted, repeated in-flight tests were conducted to make sure everything was fully operational.

In addition to more weather and flight training specifically geared toward the rigors of an Atlantic crossing and the distinct possibility that she might often be "flying blind," Amelia kept up with her other commitments. These included her lecture tours, work for the Ninety-Nines, personal appointments, book revisions, and more. G.P. had decided to wait to release *The Fun of It* until immediately after Amelia's flight. That way she could add one final chapter describing her experiences crossing the Atlantic. Knowing her plane was in good hands—and unbothered by suspicious reporters—Amelia remained calm and confident in the days before her flight.

One of the most important changes . . . was to increase the plane's fuel capacity.

Getting Underway

In order to allow Amelia to be as well-rested as possible prior to her departure, Bernt Balchen would fly her plane up to Newfoundland, with Amelia and Eddie Gorski, a mechanic, on

Amelia stands beneath the wing of her Lockheed Vega before takeoff from Harbour Grace, Newfoundland, in an effort to become the first woman to successfully fly alone across the Atlantic.

board as passengers. Since Amelia's plane had no pontoons, the landing strip at Harbour Grace was selected for the takeoff point from Newfoundland.

After receiving word that the weather looked good, the decision was made to leave Teterboro on the afternoon of May 20. Donning a yellow silk blouse, jodhpurs (a style of riding breeches), a lightweight jacket, and carrying her leather flying suit, Amelia left the Putnams' home in Rye, New York, and headed to the airfield. G.P. met her there. As husband and wife said a brief good-bye to each other, G.P. handed Amelia a twenty-dollar bill, requesting that she send a telegram home upon her arrival in Europe.

At 3:15 p.m., with little fanfare and Balchen at the helm, the plane took off and headed for St. John, Newfoundland. After spending the night there, Balchen, Amelia, and Gorski flew out the next morning, arriving in Harbour Grace at about 2 p.m. local time. Five and a half hours later, word came via telegraph that the weather looked "promising." Carrying with her some soup and canned tomato juice, Amelia climbed into her Lockheed Vega. She smiled as a reporter snapped her picture; gunned the engine; waved to Bernt Balchen, Eddie Gorski, and the small crowd that had gathered; and sped down the runway. Climbing up into the twilight, Amelia's red plane disappeared out over the water. She was on her way.

A Dangerous Flight

Knowing the difficulty of landing on unfamiliar ground in the dark, Amelia preferred to take off at sunset, fly during the night, and—with luck—reach her destination during daylight. The flight's first hour or so passed uneventfully, and the weather was calm as Amelia flew into the sunset at about twelve thousand feet. Watching the moon rise over cloud embankments, she gazed down at her instruments. "And then," she later wrote, "something happened that has never occurred in my twelve years of flying. The altimeter, the instrument which records height above the ground, failed." This was not good—especially when Amelia ran into serious weather about an hour later. Battered by wind and rain, with lightning flashes in the distance, Amelia tried to hold her course. It was, she later recalled, "the roughest air I have ever encountered while flying completely blind."

Eventually she was able to break through to clearer weather on the other side of the storm. But about four hours into the flight,

This modern altimeter shows the pilot that he or she is flying at a height of 25,000 feet above sea level. When Amelia's altimeter failed during a rainstorm, she relied on instincts and flew "blind" until the weather cleared.

she smelled burning oil and could see a small blue flame licking up through a broken welding seam in the plane's exhaust system. She later recalled deciding—if she even had a choice—that she'd rather drown than burn. Instead of turning around, flying four more hours back to Newfoundland, and trying to land there in the dark with a heavy load of fuel, she decided to continue onward to Europe.

Thick clouds soon brought an end to any visibility. Trying to climb above them to clearer skies, Amelia noticed the engine sounded sluggish. Ice had begun to form on her plane's wings and windshield. She had climbed too high. The aircraft went into a sudden spin. Trying to remain calm, Amelia did all that she could to bring the plane out of it. "How long we spun," she recalled, "I do not know." When Amelia was finally able to pull out of the spin, she could see whitecaps on the ocean waves below. If she had gone a little farther, she would have been in the Atlantic.

She later recalled deciding—if she even had a choice—that she'd rather drown than burn.

Trying to fly under the heavy clouds became next to impossible without her altimeter. When she ran into fog she could no longer chance going low, because she might crash into the water. Instead, she soared into the higher, thicker clouds, putting her instrument training to the test. According to Amelia, the newly-installed directional gyro was "a real life-saver." After the flight, she remarked that "if I had been able to see what was happening on the outside during the night I would have had heart failure then and there; but, as I could not see, I carried on." Dawn found her flying between two layers of clouds. As the higher clouds began to thin and sunlight poured through, the reflection on the lower layer was so bright that Amelia needed sunglasses.

Holding a handful of telegrams, Amelia chats with Irish locals the day after completing her successful solo flight across the Atlantic on May 21, 1932.

About ten hours after takeoff, and by her estimation two hours away from when she might first see land, Amelia reached to turn on her reserve tank of fuel and noticed that the cabin fuel gauge had begun to leak. Fuel was dripping steadily into the cockpit and onto Amelia's left shoulder, filling the cabin with fumes. By now the portion of the exhaust system with the broken weld was vibrating badly and seemed like it might not hold out much longer.

Upon sighting a small fishing boat, Amelia knew she had to be fairly close to shore. Although she had originally hoped to land in Paris—five years to the day after Lindbergh's triumphant arrival—the night she had just experienced, combined with the plane's mechanical problems, convinced her that landing at the first suitable spot made much more sense. She saw a sloping field and began her descent. Fourteen hours and fifty-six minutes after taking off from Harbour Grace, Newfoundland, Amelia's red Lockheed Vega smoothly touched down on James Gallagher's pasture outside Londonderry, Ireland. She had flown 2,026 miles across the Atlantic—alone.

CHAPTER 10

Record Setter

*Preparation, I have often said, is rightly two-thirds
of any venture.*

With her successful solo flight across the Atlantic, Amelia
was now not only the first female pilot to accomplish
this feat, but the first person—man or woman—to make
two transatlantic journeys by air. In addition to her trip
being the fastest transatlantic hop so far, Amelia had also
established a new women's record for making the longest
nonstop flight. No longer a mere passenger, she had earned
her place in the record books.

Concern for her plane kept Amelia close to James
Gallagher's farm, though she did accept a ride into
Londonderry to telephone G.P. The press soon learned of
her success, and congratulatory messages from presidents
and prime ministers began to pour into the Londonderry
telegraph office. One favorite of Amelia's was from her dry
cleaner in Rye: "KNEW YOU WOULD DO IT . . . I NEVER
LOSE A CUSTOMER."

After a well-deserved night of rest, Amelia was
persuaded by the newsreel people to put on her leather
flying suit once more, climb back into her plane, and taxi
around the meadow for a short distance. As the cameras
rolled, she emerged from the cockpit and was greeted by a
small, cheering crowd. The film was quickly circulated to
U.S. movie theaters with the message, "Journey's end . . .
here she is safe and sound on a farm in Ireland having just
completed the first flight by a woman across the Atlantic."

Recreating her arrival for newsreel cameras the morning following her history-making flight, Amelia is surrounded by well-wishers in Londonderry, Ireland, on May 22, 1932.

A mechanic arrived and cautioned Amelia against flying her plane again without repairs first being made. Instead of being fixed, the plane was dismantled and shipped over to London to be put on temporary display in Selfridges department store. Since Amelia had been unsure of the success of her flight prior to departure, she hadn't made any post-flight plans for her stay in Europe. She gratefully accepted an invitation to stay at the home of the American ambassador and flew to London on a chartered news agency plane. At Amelia's request, G.P. boarded the next ocean liner departing for Europe so that he could meet his wife in France.

As with the *Friendship* flight, Amelia again found herself without a wardrobe, but her celebrity status ensured credit was extended to her at London stores. Fashionably dressed once more, she met the Prince of Wales at St. James Palace, attended a reception at the House of Commons, received various awards and honors, was wined and dined, and gave so many speeches that her voice was little more than a whisper by the time she sailed for France on June 2. G.P. joined her in the French city of Cherbourg, and together they took a train to Paris—the original destination of her transatlantic flight.

Amelia and G.P. surrounded by well-wishers upon their arrival in Paris.

Cheered by crowds and with the additional medals and awards that had been bestowed upon her, Amelia was officially received by the French Senate—the first foreign woman to be so honored. From Paris, Amelia and G.P. traveled on to Rome and then Belgium. At last, on June 15, 1932, nearly a month after Amelia had taken off from Harbour Grace in her red Vega, she, G.P., and her carefully crated plane sailed for New York on the *Ile de France*. America was waiting for Amelia's homecoming.

On June 7, 1932, Amelia became the first foreign woman to be officially received by the French Senate. "It is far more difficult and important to make good laws than to fly the Atlantic," she told them.

Another Triumphant Return

Because the United States was struggling with the **Great Depression**, Amelia asked that celebrations be downplayed. However, Americans had had little to cheer about for quite some time and turned out in force to greet their returning heroine. Met dockside by various dignitaries as the *Ile de France* arrived in New York, Amelia was also greeted by an air show put on by Army, Navy, and National Guard pilots. After speeches, receptions, and a ticker-tape parade, G.P. and Amelia took a train to Washington, D.C., for dinner at the White House with President and Mrs. Herbert Hoover. Afterward, Amelia was presented with a special gold medal from the National Geographic Society, of which she was the first female recipient.

Celebrations continued after Amelia returned to the U.S. in mid-June. Here she waves to crowds during a ticker-tape parade in New York City.

Other receptions followed, including one in Boston that Amy and Muriel Earhart attended. In July, Amelia made two trips to California in the now fully-repaired Vega. On July 29, she was awarded the Distinguished Flying Cross by U.S. Vice President Charles Curtis. He was in California to open the Olympic Games, which Amelia also attended. The following month, on August 24, Amelia flew nonstop from Los Angeles, California, to Newark, New Jersey, the first woman pilot to do so.

Taking the First Lady for a Ride

November brought news of Franklin D. Roosevelt's election to the presidency. Shortly thereafter, Amelia and G.P. were invited to dine with the Roosevelts in their Hyde Park, New York, home and later were occasional guests once the new First Family moved into the White House. At the end of one dinner there in April of 1933, Eleanor Roosevelt expressed her interest in seeing the lights of the capital from the air.

Amelia and G.P. were frequent visitors to the Roosevelt White House. On April 30, 1933, the first lady joined Amelia for a night-flight over the nation's capital.

After calling Eastern Air Lines to make arrangements, Amelia and Mrs. Roosevelt headed to the airport. Still dressed in their elegant evening clothes, they boarded a plane and soon were aloft—it was the first time a first lady had flown at night. Accompanying them were Eleanor Roosevelt's brother Hall and several newsmen. The next day's *Washington Post* reported, "A slim, quiet woman in a white evening dress took Mrs. Roosevelt on a flight over Washington and Baltimore last night, piloting the big transport plane without even removing her long white kid gloves."

Keeping Women in the Forefront of Aviation

In the summer of 1933, Amelia and Ruth Nichols became the first women flyers to participate in the National Air Races—referred to by some as the "Kentucky Derby of the air world." While both entered the event knowing they had little chance of winning against the professional male pilots who flew much more powerful airplanes, Amelia and Ruth felt it was important that they take part in the event to promote women pilots. An added incentive was the special prize of $2,000 for the first female pilot to finish the race.

In 1933, Amelia and Ruth Nichols became the first women to compete in the National Air Races. Although she missed being first overall, Amelia still received a sizable prize as the first woman to finish the race.

Amelia came in ahead of Ruth, who had been delayed by mechanical problems. Shortly afterward, Amelia took off from Los Angeles in an attempt to better her 1932 transcontinental flight time. Arriving in Newark seventeen hours and seven minutes later, she was able to beat her earlier time by nearly two hours.

A Grueling Schedule on the Ground

Early in 1934, Amelia launched a clothing line over which she had nearly complete control. Her stylish yet practical designs were marketed in stores such as Macy's in New York and Marshall Field's in Chicago. She also continued her lecture tour schedule. Although she did fly on occasion, Amelia's preference was to arrange her speaking engagements so that she could drive from one to another.

Ruth Nichols (1901–1960)

Born in New York City, Ruth Nichols traced her interest in aviation to an airplane ride her father arranged for her when she completed high school. By 1924, this Wellesley College graduate became only the second woman to obtain a pilot's license from the U.S. Department of Commerce and the first American woman seaplane pilot. Throughout her lengthy aviation career, Ruth flew nearly every type of contemporary aircraft, including dirigibles, gliders, autogiros, amphibians, single-, twin-, and four-engine planes, as well as supersonic jets. She also became the first woman pilot to land in all the lower forty-eight states. She was a founding member of the Ninety-Nines and also organized the Relief Wings in 1939. This civilian air ambulance group later served with the Civil Air Patrol during World War II.

Ruth set many early women's aviation records, at one point becoming the only female pilot to hold the international speed, altitude, and long distance flying records all at the same time.

A magazine article details one of Ruth Nichols's two attempts to fly solo across the Atlantic. Both were unsuccessful.

"Designed for the woman who lives actively," Amelia's clothing line mirrored her own casual elegance. Some thirty department stores carried her designs, which included daily wear as well as flying apparel.

Typically, once her speech was over, she remained for a while, signing autographs, giving interviews to area papers, greeting local dignitaries, and attending small receptions. She often did not leave a lecture hall until around midnight. Rather than settle into an area hotel, she usually hopped in her car and drove on to the next stop, preferring to sleep once the drive was behind her.

In some ways, Amelia's tour schedules seemed even more grueling than her long-distance flights. In one October on the road, she gave twenty-three speeches in twenty-five days, and during another six-week period, she drove a total of seven thousand miles. Usually Amelia earned about $2,400 speaking seven or eight times in a week (about $36,000 per week in today's dollars). Public speaking rapidly became her primary source of income.

A New Plane

By this time Amelia felt she was ready for a new plane. Her trusty Lockheed Vega had been through so much that it needed a major overhaul. Rather than spend the $10,000 or so to restore it, she sold the plane to Philadelphia's Franklin Institute for $7,500 where it would be placed in a permanent aviation exhibition. (Eventually it would become part of the collection at the Smithsonian National Air and Space Museum.) Once again, Amelia selected a Lockheed Vega—this one could fly at speeds of up to two hundred miles per hour and was equipped with streamlined landing gear, special fuel tanks, and other distinctive modifications.

Amelia piloted this Lockheed Vega across the Atlantic and into the history books on May 21, 1932. Today it is on display at the Smithsonian National Air and Space Museum.

After returning from a relaxing and enjoyable Wyoming dude ranch vacation with G.P. in the summer of 1934, Amelia realized that she needed a new challenge. Although she was still very popular as a speaker, Amelia felt she was becoming slightly stale. In addition, her clothing line—while initially popular—had not been a commercial success.

Sadly, that November a fire had severely damaged Amelia and G.P.'s Rye, New York, home—destroying many of Amelia's childhood possessions. The couple began spending more and more time in California. The vast Pacific, largely unchallenged by aviators, stretched westward from the California coast, beckoning to Amelia, and she began to make plans.

Flight Across the Pacific

Rationalizing that it would be easier to find a continent than an island, Amelia planned to fly from Hawaii to California. Christmas Day, 1934, found G.P., Amelia, and Amelia's tarp-covered plane aboard the SS *Lurline*, sailing for Honolulu. When asked by reporters about her plans, Amelia—in typical fashion—

Amelia arrives in Hawaii by ship in December 1934. Her eastbound flight the following month made her the first pilot to fly solo across both the Atlantic and this stretch of the Pacific.

replied that she thought she might do some flying around the Hawaiian Islands.

Instead, on January 11, 1935, she took off from Honolulu's Wheeler Field, bound for Oakland, California, some 2,400 miles away. If successful, it would be her longest flight to date, and she would be the first pilot—male or female—to make the trip. She would also be the first to have flown across both the Atlantic and a sizable portion of the Pacific.

Taking off from the warm climate of Wheeler Field, Amelia did not have to worry about ice on her wings during the trip, but she did have a life vest and inflatable raft stowed on board. During the flight she was treated to a night of beauty. The stars, she wrote, "seemed to rise from the sea and hang outside my cockpit window, near enough to touch."

For the first time, Amelia's plane was equipped with a two-way radio—an innovation that brought her much enjoyment. She was even able to speak with G.P. when she was hundreds of miles from shore. Some radio stations were able to pick up her signal, and the public was kept informed of her progress. Nearly eighteen hours after leaving Honolulu, Amelia announced, "Am on course, will be in any moment now." After glimpsing San Francisco Bay off her wing tip,

She would also be the first to have flown across both the Atlantic and a sizable portion of the Pacific.

Departing from Honolulu on January 11, 1935, Amelia arrived in Oakland, California, more than eighteen hours later. She was the first pilot ever to fly the route solo.

she began her descent into the Oakland airfield. Thousands were there to greet her. Surprised by the size of the crowd, Amelia later commented, "I thought there might be some kind of meet going on when I first saw it."

More Record-Breaking Flights

Just three months later, Amelia again set a record—this time a double—by making the first successful solo flight from Los Angeles to Mexico City and then from Mexico City to Newark. Departing just before midnight on April 19, 1935, Amelia flew south from California for a little over thirteen hours, covering 1,700 miles. After a delay of more than two weeks in Mexico City, where she awaited an okay on the weather from expert meteorologist Doc Kimball in New York, Amelia took off again on May 9, heading to Newark some 2,185 miles to the northeast. Fourteen hours and eighteen minutes later, she was on the ground in New Jersey. In the long hours of these three flights in 1935, Amelia began to form a plan. "There was one flight which I most wanted to attempt," she wrote, "a circumnavigation of the globe as near its waistline as could be." Now approaching age forty, Amelia imagined this flight around the world would be the grand finale of her aviation career. After that there would be no major records left, and her flying would simply be for pleasure, not for setting records.

CHAPTER 11

Final Challenge

It is far easier to start something than it is to finish it.

If Amelia was going to undertake a lengthy around-the-world flight, one of the first things she needed was a new plane. Too much would be riding on this trip to fly with a single engine. Beyond the expense of the aircraft, the costs for a 27,000-mile flight would be enormous. Fuel and its storage all over the world, spare parts, repairs en route, accommodations, navigation charts—the list seemed endless, but Amelia was quietly determined. "I have a feeling there is just about one more good flight left in my system," she said, "and I hope this trip is it."

Around the same time that Amelia made her Mexico City flight during the spring of 1935, Purdue University had offered her a faculty position. Since only about

Inspecting her new Lockheed 10E Electra as it nears completion, Amelia prepares for her upcoming around-the-world flight. She knows it will be the longest and most challenging of her career.

one-fifth of Purdue's four thousand students were female, it was felt that someone like Amelia could make a difference. She accepted the offer and on September 1 joined the Purdue faculty as a consultant in careers of women. Once her appointment was announced, female student enrollment increased by fifty percent.

Not long afterward, Purdue's trustees set up a fund for aeronautical research, which matched up nicely with Amelia's still-unannounced plans for an around-the-world flight. While she was flying, she could conduct research for the university. The idea of a "flying laboratory" was born, and Amelia had just the plane in mind—the Lockheed 10E Electra. On July 24, 1936, her thirty-ninth birthday, Amelia took possession of what would be her last airplane.

Flight Plans

Plans for Amelia's historic flight quietly moved forward, with G.P. handling many of the arrangements. This in itself was a huge job. Clearances for many of the planned stops had to be obtained from both the U.S. Navy and the Bureau of Air Commerce. Permission was needed from each country Amelia would fly over in case an emergency landing was necessary.

It was also up to G.P. to reassure foreign officials that Amelia would not be carrying weapons or filming military installations from the air. Amelia would also need to be able to access weather reports as she made her way around the world. At one point she gratefully acknowledged G.P.'s contributions, saying, "I know I'm lucky to have him, for I never could do it without his help. He takes care of everything."

Even though she would be doing all the flying, Amelia realized she needed someone else on board—a well-trained navigator. Since fueling stops would all be prearranged, with

The Flying Laboratory

One of the most advanced aircraft in production at the time, the all-metal Lockheed 10E Electra was low-winged with twin engines and could carry up to ten passengers. Special modifications—including the installation of additional fuel tanks, an autopilot, a two-way radio, and a **Morse code** transmission system—brought the total delivery price for Amelia's aircraft to $42,000 (the equivalent of more than $600,000 today).

The plane's specially designed cockpit had two seats and was roughly shaped like a four-and-a-half foot cube. Amelia called it her "cubbyhole." Some fifty gauges and dials made up the instrument panel. The most important ones were mounted directly in front of her to help avoid eye strain.

In the rear of the Electra, passenger seats were removed to accommodate six fuel tanks. Behind

Space is at a premium in the crowded cockpit of Amelia's Lockheed Electra that has been outfitted with the latest state-of-the-art equipment.

the tanks was the navigator's station, where a window had been added to the cabin ceiling so the plane's course could be tracked using the position of the stars. A low, wide chart table was mounted about eighteen inches off the floor. Near it were various instruments, including a compass. The navigator and pilot would communicate by writing notes on cards, paper-clipping them to the end of a shortened bamboo fishing pole, and reeling the notes back and forth.

supplies stored in advance, she would need to reach very specific landing sites all over the world. It would be up to the navigator to make sure she was right on course. Knowing of his excellent reputation as both a navigator and a radio operator, Amelia asked Harry Manning to fly with her on the most difficult leg of the trip—across the vast expanse of the Pacific. He accepted and was able to arrange a three-month leave of absence from his job.

A second relief navigator was also employed—Fred Noonan. Once a highly respected navigator for Pan American World Airways, Noonan had had some problems with alcohol. These seemed to be behind him, however, and Amelia felt confident he could do the job. Finally, Paul Mantz, a skilled pilot who was well versed in the latest aviation technology, was hired as the technical advisor for the flight. He gave Amelia additional training in long-range flying and offered instruction for sharpening her navigation skills.

It would be up to the navigator to make sure she was right on course.

In February of 1937, Amelia was ready to publicly announce her plans. Newsmen made notes and took photos while she used a globe to detail her planned route—California to Hawaii, Hawaii to Howland Island in the Pacific, from there onto

Amelia poses with her original around-the-world team. Standing with her (from left to right) are technical advisor Paul Mantz and navigators Harry Manning and Fred Noonan.

All agreed that the most difficult leg of Amelia's flight would be reaching tiny Howland Island. Only two miles from end to end, it could be easy to miss in the vast Pacific.

Australia, then Africa, Arabia, and across the southern Atlantic Ocean to Brazil before heading northward back to the U.S. When asked how long the trip would take, Amelia replied, "I'm simply going to fly as and when I can, race nothing and nobody."

Of all the planned stops, Howland Island in the Central Pacific caused the most concern. Only two miles long and a half-mile wide with a maximum elevation of just twenty feet, Howland was just a tiny dot in the enormous ocean. To find it would be extremely challenging, but there was no way Amelia could cross the Pacific without refueling. Harry Manning assured her he could locate it. Since they were heading there at the beginning of the trip, both he and Amelia would be well rested and up for the challenge.

An Ominous False Start

On March 17, 1937, Amelia set off from Oakland, bound for Honolulu. On board were Fred Noonan and Harry Manning. Noonan would fly with Amelia and Manning from Honolulu to Howland and return to the U.S. by ship. Harry Manning would stay on board all the way across the Pacific to Australia. From there Amelia would continue the rest of the way alone. Paul Mantz had also come along on the flight to Hawaii—reportedly to make one last technical check of the aircraft, but primarily to meet up with his fiancée in Honolulu. The fifteen-hour-and-forty-seven-minute flight went smoothly and even set a new speed record. The Electra arrived at Pearl Harbor's Luke Field only five minutes off Amelia's preflight estimate, prompting G.P. to joke in a telegram, "PLEASE TRY TO BE MORE EXACT."

At daybreak on March 20, Amelia, Harry, and Fred boarded the Electra for the flight to Howland Island. After taxiing out to the northeast end of the airfield, Amelia's plane roared down the runway toward takeoff. Suddenly the aircraft swung slightly right, then left. With a shower of sparks, the right-hand landing gear collapsed! The plane's heavy load may have contributed to the equipment failure.

Of all the planned stops, Howland Island in the Central Pacific caused the most concern.

Amelia calmly shut down the engines to prevent fire and went out to survey the damage. It was dreadful—and completely

Mechanics study Amelia's damaged plane after equipment failure doomed her takeoff from Hawaii on March 20, 1937. Significant repairs meant reorganizing her original globe-encircling route.

unexpected. There was nothing to do but return to California and start again.

Dismantled, crated, and shipped, the Electra arrived back at Lockheed for repairs. Meanwhile, Amelia and G.P. faced not only the enormous task of rescheduling everything, but also the costly expenses involved. It would be at least three months before Amelia could take off again. Lockheed's bill alone eventually came to $14,000 (nearly $200,000 today). "To keep going I more-or-less mortgaged the future," Amelia wrote. "Without regret, however, for what are futures for?"

Reversing the Flight Direction

The delay meant completely reversing the flight's direction due to weather concerns. In order to try to avoid the start of Asia's **monsoon** season, Amelia would need to fly west-to-east. Unfortunately, Harry Manning had to return to his job, and Amelia also parted company with Paul Mantz. The difficult Pacific stretch would now come at the end of the trip, so Fred Noonan would accompany Amelia for the entire flight. From now on it would be just the two of them.

With Manning's departure, Amelia decided to have the Morse code equipment removed from the plane. She was very conscious of anything that added weight to the Electra— particularly after the failed takeoff in Honolulu. Since neither she nor Fred was skilled at using it, she did not want to carry equipment that seemed unnecessary. Amelia also felt she would not need the cumbersome long-distance radio antenna. She was confident that she would remain close enough to land to establish some sort of radio contact without having to reel out the 250-foot trailing antenna. These decisions may have been fatal errors.

CHAPTER 12

Almost

When I go, I'd like best to go in my plane. Quickly.

On the afternoon of May 21, 1937, at 3:50 p.m., Amelia took off from Oakland, California, and officially began her around-the-world flight. It had been five years since she had crossed the Atlantic on her own. Now she faced her most difficult challenge. G.P. accompanied Amelia as she flew across the U.S. Neither knew it would be their last flight together. After overnight stops in Tucson, Arizona, and New Orleans, Louisiana, the Electra continued on to Florida's Miami Municipal Airport, arriving Sunday afternoon, May 23.

There mechanics spent a final week servicing the aircraft and readying it for departure. Always low-key in front of reporters, Amelia made her public good-bye to G.P. a brief one. Recalling the moment later, G.P. would write that "her eyes were clear with the light of adventure that lay ahead." With Fred seated at his navigator's post, Amelia signaled to have the blocks holding the plane's wheels removed and taxied the aircraft to the southeastern end of the runway. With the engines smoothly purring, the Electra rose into the air a half-minute later. It was just before 6 a.m., June 1, 1937.

Flying Over South America and Africa

Arriving in Puerto Rico about eight hours later, Amelia and Fred spent the night and then flew on to Caripito, Venezuela, the following day. The next leg of the trip took them to Paramaribo (in present-day Suriname), and then it

Amelia snaps photos at the airport in Caripito, Venezuela, during the South American leg of her around-the-world flight. A few days later she would cross the Atlantic, bound for Africa.

was onward across open sea and dense jungle to Fortaleza in northeastern Brazil. There they stopped for a few days to have the Electra serviced before the long flight across the South Atlantic to Africa. During their wait, Amelia and Fred repacked the plane, sending any already-used maps and charts home.

They continued this downsizing as they traveled around the globe. Various notes, cables, filled logbooks, letters, and phone calls kept G.P. up-to-date on their progress and also formed the basis for Amelia's book about the trip. Begun as *World Flight*, the volume would eventually be published as *Last Flight*.

After a short 270-mile hop to Natal, also in Brazil, Amelia and Fred left South America behind. Crossing the equator for the second time, the Electra arrived in St. Louis, Senegal, on June 7 after some thirteen hours in the air. Dakar, 163 miles to the south, had been their planned destination, but thick haze and a miscommunication with Fred made that city impossible for Amelia to find. With darkness rapidly approaching, she made the decision to land and fly on to Dakar the next day. From Dakar they headed to Gao in French Sudan (now Mali). "As always, we found my usual calling cards," wrote Amelia, "fifty-gallon drums of gasoline, each with my name printed large upon it in white or red lettering." After sleeping in the open desert to avoid the oppressive heat, Amelia and Fred rose at dawn and continued across Central Africa.

With a toothy grin, Amelia climbs out of her cockpit in Dakar, then capital of French West Africa. After a delicious dinner, Amelia and Fred were overnight guests of the governor-general.

The Monsoons in Southeast Asia

By June 15 they were in Karachi (in today's Pakistan). Typical of everywhere they landed, the two Americans were greeted with warm and friendly hospitality. They had been traveling for eighteen days and were slightly more than halfway around the globe. Fred wrote to his wife, "Amelia is a grand person for such a trip. . . . In addition to being a fine companion and pilot, she can take hardship as well as a man—and work like one."

From Karachi it was on to Calcutta, a distance of nearly 1,400 miles. Heavy rain made the Electra almost invisible as it touched down on June 17. Amelia and Fred had hoped to avoid the beginning of monsoon season, but they were out of luck. More rain was on the way. Worried that the Calcutta airfield might soon become waterlogged and impossible to use, Amelia and Fred flew out the next day for Rangoon, Burma. After a brief refueling stop in Akyab (present-day Sittwe), they pressed on. More heavy rain and strong winds soon battered the plane, and Amelia was forced to turn around and head back to Akyab.

Well shaded by their broad-brimmed hats, Amelia and Fred pose in Karachi two weeks after their Miami departure. Travel across India was plagued by heavy rains and strong winds.

On June 19 they started out again—this time hoping to bypass Rangoon and continue ahead to Bangkok, Thailand. They hit bad weather once more and ended up in Rangoon after all. Reporting on a sightseeing drive they took during their stay, Amelia noted that "women in general here seem to have more freedom and education than in most places we have been. Many are in business and they have had a vote for many years."

Flying in cloudy skies, Amelia and Fred next headed to Bangkok where Amelia pronounced the airport among the best they had

Amelia and Fred had hoped to avoid the beginning of monsoon season, but they were out of luck.

encountered so far. Then it was on to Singapore and West Java's Bandung, where the pair climbed to the rim of an active volcano. On the flight there, the Electra had made its third pass across the equator.

Heading for Australia and Howland Island

On June 24 Amelia and Fred prepared to depart for Australia's Port Darwin. A problem with the long-range navigation instruments delayed their departure until late in the afternoon. But after a false start with the instruments still not operating properly, they were back in Bandung. Finally, on June 27, repairs were completed. Before departing, Amelia spoke to G.P. regarding the rest of the flight. She thought she'd be back in Oakland no later than June 30, and definitely hoped to be at home for the Fourth of July. It is believed to have been their final conversation.

On the way to Port Darwin, Fred set a course for a quick refueling stop on the southern tip of the island of Timor. Since they had departed late from Bandung, Amelia made the decision to stay overnight there rather than continue on to Australia that evening. Conditions in Timor were very primitive, with no airport and little in the way of accommodations. The food, however, was "astonishingly splendid," Fred wrote to his wife. After staking down the plane and covering the propellers and engine, they took a short sightseeing drive before spending the night in a government guest house.

Departing at 5 a.m. on June 28, the Electra reached Port Darwin—and the fifth continent of the trip—in three and a half hours. Thinking about the long flight ahead across the Pacific, Amelia and Fred once again took stock of the plane's contents and sent more items home. Included in the shipment were their parachutes. "A parachute," Amelia matter-of-factly noted, "would not help over the Pacific." Before tackling the vast blue ocean, they had just one more scheduled stop: Lae, New Guinea.

She thought she'd be back in Oakland no later than June 30 . . .

Once Amelia and Fred reached Lae, they had been traveling for forty days and were nearly three-quarters of the way around the globe. Only two stops remained—Howland Island and Honolulu, Hawaii, where they would be back on American soil. G.P. had already notified the press of approximately when the Electra was due back in Oakland.

Landing in Lae on June 29, Amelia's thoughts were likely focused on the thousands of miles of ocean ahead. Her final entry

Amelia's plane rests on the airfield at Port Darwin, Australia, the last refueling stop before Lae, New Guinea. The Lockheed Electra had now touched down on five continents.

in *Last Flight* reads, "the whole width of the world has passed behind us—except this broad ocean. I shall be glad when we have the hazards of its navigation behind us." The flight of more than two thousand five hundred miles to Howland would be the longest Amelia—or her plane—had ever flown in a single hop.

Knowing that it was absolutely essential that they reach the small island in daylight, the time set for their Lae departure was critical. In addition to factoring in weather information, Amelia also had to allow for the fact that they would be crossing the **International Date Line** as well as traveling through two time zones. They would, in a sense, be flying backward in time. But, unbeknownst to both Amelia and Fred, their time—no matter how it was calculated—was running out.

"A parachute," Amelia matter-of-factly noted, "would not help over the Pacific."

The Last Takeoff

Lae's thousand-yard dirt runway ended at a twenty-five-foot drop-off to the water below. As Amelia headed down its length on the morning of July 2, 1937, her plane was burdened with its heaviest load of fuel to date—some one thousand gallons, assumed to be enough for four thousand miles of flying in reasonably good conditions. Some witnessing the takeoff wondered if the Electra would make it. With fewer than fifty yards to go, the aircraft finally lifted off the ground with a high bounce and headed over the edge of the cliff. Although remaining airborne, Amelia's plane dropped to just a few feet above the sea, its propellers sending up sprays of water before it slowly began to climb.

Information about Amelia and Fred's remaining hours has been pieced together by combining details from a variety of sources.

Broadcasting with the radio **call letters** KHAQQ, Amelia planned to transmit information about the progress of her flight at fifteen and forty-five minutes after each hour. She would listen for messages on the hour and half hour. The Coast Guard cutter *Itasca* was standing by Howland's northeastern side, ready to send out radio signals. Once it was determined that Amelia was within

Shown dockside in Honolulu, the U.S. Coast Guard cutter *Itasca* was ordered to Howland Island in 1937 to await Amelia's arrival. Radio operators on board stood ready to monitor her broadcasts.

radio range, the *Itasca* would send out weather information and homing signals.

For the first third of the flight, Amelia's radio transmissions and flight data were fairly routine and heard by various radio operators in that part of the western Pacific region. Still within sight of numerous outer islands, navigation would have been fairly simple using the charts and maps on board the Electra. As the hours of the flight increased, though, one factor became increasing apparent from Amelia's transmissions—the plane was making less progress than anticipated. Strong headwinds were likely slowing its travel speed. Amelia's fuel supply would be dangerously low as she neared Howland Island.

Whether by coincidence or intentionally, U.S.-directed contractors had completed Howland's new airfield only months before as a mid-ocean refueling stop for transpacific flights. Stored there were eighteen drums of aviation fuel specifically set aside for Amelia's next hop to the Hawaiian Islands. The Howland airfield's runways had been marked with red flags, and a small guesthouse

On Howland Island, crews prepared for the Electra's arrival. Three runways were marked with red flags, and a small guesthouse had been cleaned and furnished for Amelia's comfort.

was outfitted for Amelia, her bed already made. Everything was set for her arrival.

Based upon Amelia's flight plan, it was assumed that she would be within radio transmission range of Howland around dawn. In addition to the *Itasca's* radio operators on standby, a new high frequency experimental direction finder had recently been installed on the island to pick up distant radio signals. Unfortunately, neither would be of any help to Amelia and Fred. Unbeknownst to those waiting at Howland, Amelia had removed her plane's 250-foot trailing antenna wire before departing from Miami. Always mindful of added weight that could be replaced by much-needed fuel, Amelia felt the playing out and reeling in of the antenna wire would be too much trouble in flight. She also mistakenly believed the lengthy antenna would be of little use. Removing it may have sealed her fate.

The Final Transmissions

Fourteen hours and fifteen minutes into the flight, the *Itasca* received its first radio communication from Amelia. Following heavy static, her calm voice came through saying, ". . . cloudy and overcast." The rest of her message was lost in static and no more was heard for another hour. The plane was still far from Howland, so this was no cause for concern. The next broadcast, made on schedule at fifteen minutes past the hour, came through fairly clear: "*Itasca* from Earhart. Over . . . will listen on hour and half hour on 3105." (The latter was a reference to the radio frequency of 3105 **kilocycles** that Amelia was using to transmit and receive her messages.) In response, the *Itasca* radioman gave details on the weather, acknowledged receiving her message, and asked her to report in again with details of her position at her next scheduled transmission time—at fifteen minutes before the hour.

When nothing was heard from Amelia at her next two scheduled transmission times, the radioman repeated his earlier message on the hour and the half hour as planned. Not long after, another message came in from Amelia, but the transmission was so faint and had so much static that it was impossible to decipher. About seventeen hours into the flight, Amelia was briefly heard again requesting information on the 3105 kilocycle frequency and noting that she was "about 200 miles out."

She . . . believed the lengthy antenna would be of little use. Removing it may have sealed her fate.

Her next transmission came through on schedule at fifteen minutes past the hour: "Please take bearing on us and report in half hour I will make noise in microphone about 100 miles out." Amelia whistled, but the transmission cut off before any sort of signal could be traced. Dawn broke thirty minutes later at Howland.

By this time Amelia and Fred should have had a good chance of seeing the island and the *Itasca*—which was sending a steady column of black smoke into the relatively still air—if they were as close as Amelia had indicated. That they were not became clear in Amelia's next message—received nineteen hours into the flight: "We must be on you but cannot see you but gas is running low have been unable to reach you by radio we are flying at 1,000 feet." At this point, the radio personnel on the *Itasca* opted to drop the agreed-upon schedule. They would transmit—and hopefully receive—continuously.

Nearly a half hour later came another message: "We are circling but cannot see island cannot hear you go ahead on 7500 kilocycles with long count either now or on schedule time on half hour." Perhaps in desperation—for Amelia had no way of knowing if her messages were being received—she was asking to change broadcast frequencies. The *Itasca* responded on both frequencies.

By now tension was building rapidly in the radio room, so it was with great relief that they heard the next message: "KHAQQ calling *Itasca*. We received your signals but unable to get a minimum please take bearings on us and answer on 3105 kilocycles." It was the only time two-way communication was confirmed between Amelia and the *Itasca*. Unfortunately, the quality of the transmission was so poor that neither could get a bearing on the other. Regardless, the radio operators on the *Itasca* continued to try to reach Amelia using several different frequencies and transmitting nearly continuously.

Finally, after having spent more than twenty hours in the air, Amelia's voice came through once more: "We are on the line of position 157 dash 337 will repeat this message on 6210 kilocycles. We are now running north and south." And that . . . was all.

The press and public continued to hold out hope that Amelia and Fred would be found in the days following their disappearance.

CHAPTER 13

Lost, but Not Forgotten

I think probably . . . that I'll not live—to be old.

Continuing to transmit after Amelia's final message, the *Itasca* waited . . . and waited. After ninety minutes, with no further message received, the first word went out that her plane might be down. It had been nearly twenty-two hours since the Electra had taken off from the Lae airfield. Even under the best flying conditions, time had simply run out. Amelia had endured so much and overcome so many obstacles that it seemed inconceivable to many that she might be gone. In addition to her friendship with America's president and first lady, Amelia was an international celebrity, beloved around the world.

So began one of the most intensive—and expensive—sea and air searches ever undertaken up to that date in history. In all, more than $4 million was reportedly spent by the federal government trying to locate the Electra and its crew (more than $56 million today). Ships and planes scoured miles of the Pacific and its tiny, uninhabited islands. The initial search, which

Hoping for word of their aunt's fate, Amelia's nephew and niece—David and Amy Morrissey—stay tuned to radio broadcasts at their Massachusetts home.

focused on an area relatively close to Howland, soon expanded to a grid covering tens of thousands of square miles.

G.P., who had been waiting at the Coast Guard station in San Francisco, was stunned by the news that Amelia and Fred were missing. Even so, he optimistically noted that the plane's large wings and empty fuel tanks should help to keep it afloat. On board were a two-person life raft, life belts, flares, a signal kite, and emergency water and rations. Amelia had kept a cool head in other difficult situations; surely she would come through this one, too.

Telling reporters that he still believed his wife might be stranded on a desert island, G.P. returned to New Jersey from California for a frustrating wait for further news.

Spending sleepless days and nights hoping for word that his wife and her navigator had been found, G.P. called everyone he could think of in government and business to help in some way with the search. Speaking of Amelia to a reporter, he said, "She has more courage than anyone I know. I am worried, of course, but I have confidence in her ability to handle any situation." Although doubters may previously have looked upon G.P.'s role in Amelia's life as merely that of a manager or promoter, his love for her was painfully obvious as he waited for news.

Dwindling Hope

As the days and weeks passed, mail sent by Amelia from stops along her around-the-world route continued to arrive. Letters, logbooks, jotted notes, even a birthday gift for her niece were all bittersweet reminders of what was lost. On July 18 the search around Howland Island was called off, and by month's end the official report concluded that the Electra had crashed into the sea with Amelia and Fred on board. Despite G.P.'s insistence that the plane would probably float, the likelihood of their survival now seemed impossible. But G.P. and others continued to hope.

After posting a sizable reward for any information about the plane's disappearance, G.P. was contacted by psychics, soothsayers, swindlers, and the mentally ill in the weeks and years following Amelia's disappearance—all supposedly having proof of her survival. Amelia and Fred were marooned on a desert island. They had been seen living elsewhere under different names. They were on a spying mission for the U.S. government and had been captured by the Japanese. This last theory persisted for many years—especially in light of Japan's bombing of Pearl Harbor just four years after Amelia's flight.

G.P. pursued all reasonable—and some unreasonable—clues. Perhaps longer than anyone else, Amy Earhart held out hope for Amelia's safe return. For years she kept a packed suitcase ready in case she needed to travel to her rescued daughter's side. But no certifiable trace of the Electra or its occupants has ever been found. On January 5, 1939, Amelia Earhart was declared legally dead.

Throughout Amelia's around-the-world flight, Amy Earhart listened to radio broadcasts of her famous daughter's progress. For many years, Amy remained unshaken in her belief that Amelia would be found.

Last Flight Repeated

In 1997, veteran pilot and Texas businesswoman Linda Finch became the first to successfully complete Amelia Earhart's around-the-equator route in a plane nearly identical to that of the famous flyer. Piloting her restored Lockheed 10E Electra some 26,000 miles in ten weeks, Finch stopped in twenty countries on five continents along the way. Her trip around the globe took longer than it would have in a modern plane due to the difficulty of finding the proper fuel for the historic aircraft. Although Finch's plane was equipped with much more sophisticated navigation and communication aids, the Electra's non-pressurized cabin and lack of oxygen equipment duplicated the conditions under which Amelia had flown.

Linda Finch waves from outside the cockpit of her restored Lockheed 10E Electra after successfully duplicating—and completing—Amelia's 1937 flight.

A $4.5 million grant made the recreated flight possible. Passing over tiny Howland Island sixty years after Amelia's disappearance, Finch dropped three wreaths from her plane in remembrance.

Even though more than seventy years have passed since Amelia Earhart's disappearance, the question of what really happened to the famous flyer and her navigator is still the subject of research and wonder. A host of books has been written detailing a variety of theories. The most widely accepted belief, however, is that due to either an error in navigation or piloting, the Electra flew off course, ran out of fuel, and was forced down.

Whether the plane crashed or somehow made a water landing, Amelia and Fred no doubt died somewhere in the Pacific—probably not all that far from Howland Island. The problems that Fred experienced with the Electra's long-range navigation instruments before the Australia leg of the trip might have resurfaced. Or, just as the *Friendship* crew had missed seeing Ireland when crossing the Atlantic in 1928, perhaps Amelia and Fred had been unable to spot tiny Howland Island as they flew across the vast Pacific.

Perhaps longer than anyone else, Amy Earhart held out hope for Amelia's safe return.

Many who have studied the known details of the flight believe the pair was not that far off course, and some of the more recent **salvage** efforts to find the Electra's remains have been based in the vicinity of its original Howland destination.

The Legacy She Left Behind

Regardless of Amelia's fate, what is more important is the legacy she left behind.

Daring to take on new challenges, she offered living proof to the women of her day that no achievement was unattainable. Her spirit, poise, grace, and heroism are still admired more than a century after her birth, and her contributions to the field of aviation remain invaluable.

In today's world of easy, climate-controlled continent-to-continent travel, it is hard to imagine the risks and dangers Amelia faced each time she sat in the cockpit of a plane. Newsreel footage shows her easy grace as she climbs up onto the wing of her plane—then a pleasant smile, a friendly wave, and a simple farewell. For those to whom she still serves as an inspiration, Amelia Earhart will always remain young, lovely, and eager for the next great adventure.

Fewer than five months before her disappearance over the Pacific Ocean, Amelia Earhart stands with arms outstretched in front of her Lockheed Electra—the last plane she would ever fly.

Glossary

aerial advertising—skywriting and flying with banners.

aerodynamics—how air interacts with moving objects (such as airplanes).

airspeed—the speed of an object in relation to the surrounding air.

Armistice Day—the anniversary of the date when the agreement was signed to end World War I.

bloomer[s]—loose pants gathered at the knee and worn by women for active play.

byline—a line at the start of a newspaper or magazine article giving the author's name.

call letters—the identifying letters or numbers for a radio transmitting station.

chauvinistic—the attitude that members of one sex are better than another.

claims agent—someone who handles demands or requests for money or payment.

coming-out ball—a social debut or presentation of a young girl.

edicts—commands or public statements from someone with authority.

finishing school—a girls' private school stressing social and cultural training.

fuselage—the body of an aircraft.

Great Depression—a period in U.S. history marked by serious economic failure and unemployment.

International Date Line—an imaginary line, running from the North to the South Pole in roughly the middle of the Pacific Ocean, that separates one calendar day from the next.

kilocycle—1,000 cycles per second (used as a radio frequency).

launch—a small motorboat used for short-distance transportation.

monsoon—a wind system that brings very heavy rainfall to southern Asia.

Morse code—a system of dots and dashes, or long and short sounds, used to transmit messages.

patron—one who gives generous support or approval.

salvage—recovery of sunken or wrecked ships or aircraft.

settlement house—an institution that provides assistance and community services to a city's heavily populated, lower-income area.

ticker tape—the paper ribbon from a telegraphic machine that prints out stock quotes or news information; often used in parades honoring heroes.

Volunteer Aid Detachment—an organization that coordinated the work of volunteers in British hospitals.

World's Fair—a large exhibition of agricultural and industrial products, arts and crafts, and scientific advances from around the world.

Bibliography

Books

Backus, Jean L. *Letters From Amelia*. Boston: Beacon Press, 1982.

Burke, John. *Flying Solo*. New York: Sterling Publishing Co., Inc., 2007.

Butler, Susan. *East to the Dawn: The Life of Amelia Earhart*. New York: Da Capo Press, Inc., 1997.

Earhart, Amelia. *The Fun of It*. Chicago: Academy Chicago Publishers, 1977.

Earhart, Amelia. *Last Flight*. New York: Orion Books, 1988.

Goldstein, Donald M. and Katherine V. Dillon. *Amelia: The Centennial Biography of an Aviation Pioneer*. Washington: Brassey's, Inc., 1997.

Lovell, Mary S. *The Sound of Wings*. New York: St. Martin's Press, 1989.

Lubben, Kristen and Erin Barnett, eds. *Amelia Earhart: Image and Icon*. New York: International Center of Photography, 2007.

Morrissey, Muriel Earhart and Carol L. Osborne. *Amelia, My Courageous Sister*. Santa Clara, CA: Osborne Publisher, Inc., 1987.

Putnam, George Palmer. *Soaring Wings*. New York: Harcourt, Brace and Company, 1939.

Stone, Tanya Lee. *Amelia Earhart*. New York: DK Publishing, 2007.

Videotape

The American Experience: *Amelia Earhart—The Price of Courage*, 1993.

Web sites

Amelia Earhart collection at Purdue University: http://www.lib.purdue.edu/spcol/aearhart/

Official Amelia Earhart website: http://www.ameliaearhart.com/about/quotes.html

"Profit With Honor." *Time*, 4/20/1931, online at
http://www.time.com/time/magazine/article/0,9171,741465,00.html

Railey, Hilton H. "Preface to Greatness." *San Francisco Chronicle*, 9/11/1938, online at
http://www.sfmuseum.org/hist6/amelia3.html

Source Notes

The following list identifies the sources of the quoted material found in this book. The first and last few words of each quotation are cited, followed by the source. Complete information on each source can be found in the Bibliography.

Abbreviations:

AE—Official Amelia Earhart Web site

AMCS—*Amelia, My Courageous Sister*

CENT—*Amelia: The Centennial Biography of an Aviation Pioneer*

EAST—*East to the Dawn: The Life of Amelia Earhart*

FLY—*Flying Solo*

FUN—*The Fun of It*

IMAGE—*Amelia Earhart: Image and Icon*

KIM—"Profit With Honor." *Time*

LAST—*Last Flight*

LTRS—*Letters from Amelia*

NEWS—The American Experience: *Amelia Earhart—The Price of Courage*

PREF—"Preface to Greatness." *San Francisco Chronicle*

SOUND—*The Sound of Wings*

STONE—*Amelia Earhart*

WINGS—*Soaring Wings*

INTRODUCTION: Woman of Courage

> **PAGE 1** *"Courage . . . for granting peace.":* EAST, p. 131

> **PAGE 1** *"Women must try . . . challenge to others.":* LAST, p. 134

PAGE 57 *"I was just baggage . . . potatoes."*: CENT, p. 54
PAGES 57–58 *"I WISH TO EXPRESS . . . FLIGHT."*: CENT, p. 58
PAGE 58 *"SUCCESS . . . MR. STULTZ."*: CENT, p. 58
PAGE 58 *"Maybe some day . . . it alone."*: CENT, p. 54
PAGE 60 *"the kind of face . . . everybody,"*: CENT, p. 55
PAGE 60 *"I have never apologized . . . in my life."*: CENT, p. 55
PAGE 61 *"To Amelia . . . your stick forward."*: EAST, p. 212
PAGE 64 *"Flying with me . . . in the business."*: EAST, p. 336
PAGE 65 *"The tapering loveliness . . . things she did."*: WINGS, p. 215
PAGE 65 *"Your hats . . . them at all!"*: WINGS, p. 78

CHAPTER 8: Marriage and More
PAGE 66 *"I knew I had found . . . put up with me."*: WINGS, p. 154
PAGE 67 *"We are still trying . . . just 'pilots.'"*: FUN, p. 152
PAGE 69 *"a chance to play . . . not as women."*: EAST, p. 230
PAGE 69 *"to provide a close relationship . . . in general."*: EAST, p. 233
PAGE 71 *"DAD'S LAST BIG CASE . . . WITHOUT PAIN."*: AMCS, p. 113
PAGE 71 *"There is no reason . . . show ability."*: EAST, p. 240
PAGE 73 *"You must know . . . best in every way."*: WINGS, p. 76

CHAPTER 9: Atlantic Solo
PAGE 74 *"I chose to fly . . . because I wanted to."*: FUN, p. 210
PAGE 74 *"whether I flew it or it flew me."*: FUN, p. 133
PAGE 76 *"clutch at the heart"*: WINGS, p. 99
PAGE 76 *"don't issue edicts . . . from experience,"*: FUN, p. 100
PAGE 80 *"promising."*: EAST, p. 267
PAGE 80 *"And then something . . . above the ground, failed."*: FUN, p. 214
PAGE 80 *"the roughest air . . . flying completely blind."*: AMCS, p. 124
PAGE 81 *"How long we spun I do not know."*: WINGS, p. 108
PAGE 81 *"a real life-saver."*: FUN, p. 215
PAGE 81 *"if I had been able . . . I carried on."*: AMCS, p. 125

CHAPTER 10: Record Setter
PAGE 83 *"Preparation . . . two-thirds of any venture."*: LAST, p. 27
PAGE 83 *"KNEW YOU WOULD DO IT . . . CUSTOMER."*: LTRS, p. 127
PAGE 83 *"Journey's end . . . across the Atlantic."*: NEWS
PAGE 85 *"It is far more . . . fly the Atlantic,"*: CENT, p. 105
PAGE 87 *"A slim, quiet woman . . . white kid gloves."*: FLY, p. 94
PAGE 87 *"Kentucky Derby of the air world."*: IMAGE, p. 29
PAGE 90 *"Designed for the woman who lives actively,"*: EAST, p. 299
PAGE 92 *"seemed to rise from the sea . . . to touch."*: AMCS, p. 155
PAGE 92 *"Am on course . . . moment now."*: WINGS, p. 263
PAGE 93 *"I thought . . . I first saw it."*: EAST, p. 328
PAGE 93 *"There was one . . . as could be."*: LAST, p. 2

CHAPTER 11: Final Challenge
PAGE 94 *"It is far easier . . . to finish it."*: AE
PAGE 94 *"I have a feeling . . . this trip is it."*: STONE, p. 105
PAGE 95 *"I know I'm lucky . . . care of everything."*: CENT, p. 169
PAGE 96 *"cubbyhole."*: LAST, p. 12
PAGE 98 *"I'm simply going to fly . . . and nobody."*: CENT, p. 166
PAGE 99 *"PLEASE TRY TO BE MORE EXACT."*: EAST, p. 381
PAGE 100 *"To keep going . . . what are futures for?"*: LAST, p. 43

CHAPTER 12: Almost
PAGE 101 *"When I go, I'd like best . . . Quickly."*: LAST, p. xvii
PAGE 101 *"her eyes were clear . . . lay ahead."*: WINGS, p. 290
PAGE 102 *"As always . . . in white or red lettering."*: LAST, p. 85
PAGE 103 *"Amelia is a grand person . . . work like one."*: LAST, p. 51, footnote
PAGE 104 *"women in general . . . for many years."*: LAST, p. 118

Image Credits

About the Author

Author **Victoria Garrett Jones** says, "I read my first Amelia Earhart biography at the age of ten and was forever hooked—both by the fascinating woman and the unsolved mystery. In 1986, while I was on staff at the National Geographic Society, word came that Dr. Robert Ballard and his associates had found the remains of the RMS *Titanic*. One of my first thoughts was that perhaps *now* someone might also be able to find Amelia's plane. But the vast Pacific is littered with the remains of hundreds of aircraft from the battles of World War II. What chance is there that the Electra might be found? Perhaps, in this age where there are fewer and fewer unknowns, it is better that Amelia's fate remains forever a mystery."

Jones is a freelance writer and former National Geographic Society researcher; she lives with her husband and two children on Maryland's Eastern Shore. This is her seventh publication for Sterling.

Index

Discover interesting personalities
in the Sterling Biographies® series:

Marian Anderson: *A Voice Uplifted*
Neil Armstrong: *One Giant Leap for Mankind*
Alexander Graham Bell: *Giving Voice to the World*
Cleopatra: *Egypt's Last and Greatest Queen*
Christopher Columbus: *The Voyage That Changed the World*
Jacques Cousteau: *A Life Under the Sea*
Davy Crockett: *Frontier Legend*
Marie Curie: *Mother of Modern Physics*
Frederick Douglass: *Rising Up from Slavery*
Amelia Earhart: *A Life in Flight*
Thomas Edison: *The Man Who Lit Up the World*
Albert Einstein: *The Miracle Mind*
Anne Frank: *Hidden Hope*
Benjamin Franklin: *Revolutionary Inventor*
Matthew Henson: *The Quest for the North Pole*
Harry Houdini: *Death-Defying Showman*
Thomas Jefferson: *Architect of Freedom*
Joan of Arc: *Heavenly Warrior*
Helen Keller: *Courage in Darkness*
John F. Kennedy: *Voice of Hope*
Martin Luther King, Jr.: *A Dream of Hope*
Lewis & Clark: *Blazing a Trail West*
Abraham Lincoln: *From Pioneer to President*
Rosa Parks: *Courageous Citizen*
Eleanor Roosevelt: *A Courageous Spirit*
Franklin Delano Roosevelt: *A National Hero*
Harriet Tubman: *Leading the Way to Freedom*
George Washington: *An American Life*
The Wright Brothers: *First in Flight*
Malcolm X: *A Revolutionary Voice*